PRAISE FOR TWO-COMMA WEALTH

"Every so often, you come across someone who just thinks differently. George Stefanou is one of those rare professionals. In *Two-Comma Wealth*, he delivers a practical, insightful, and values-driven approach to managing significant wealth. He simplifies complexity, aligns wealth with purpose, and helps readers navigate the evolving financial landscape."

> — Libby Griewe, host of *The Efficient Advisor* podcast and financial planning consultant

"While many personal finance books focus on how to accumulate wealth, few discuss what to do once financial independence is achieved. *Two-Comma Wealth* fills this gap, offering an excellent guide for investors with substantial assets."

> — *BlueInk Review*[1]

"A holistic money management guide for those with multimillion-dollar net worths. *Two-Comma Wealth* assesses what wealth is for and how it can enrich a life, describes the effort and expertise responsible wealth management requires, and explores financial pitfalls that can ensnare the inexperienced millionaire."

> — *Foreword Reviews*[2]

"Stefanou writes with empathy while offering advice that will guide readers to responsible financial behavior. . . . The book provides a solid base of information, enriched by anonymized stories from clients' adventures in saving, investing, and bequeathing inheritances."

> — *Kirkus Reviews*[3]

---

[1] Read the full review at *BlueInk Review* (blueinkreview.com).
[2] Read the full review at *Foreword Reviews* (forewordreviews.com).
[3] Read the full review at *Kirkus Reviews* (kirkusreviews.com).

Two-Comma Wealth

Two-Comma Wealth

Investment, Tax, and Estate Strategies to Consider
When Your Net Worth Exceeds a Million Dollars

George Stefanou

TWO-COMMA WEALTH
Investment, Tax, and Estate Strategies to Consider When Your Net Worth Exceeds a Million Dollars

Copyright © 2025 by George Stefanou

Interior Layout and Design by Stephanie Anderson
Book Cover Design by Abigael Elliott

ISBNs:
979-8-89165-176-0 *Paperback*
979-8-89165-177-7 *Hardback*
979-8-89165-175-3 *E-book*

Published by:
Streamline Books
Kansas City, MO
streamlinebookspublishing.com

Streamline
BOOKS

To my mom and dad, who fostered my love for finance and showed me the value of hard work;

To my wife, Kristin, for her unwavering trust and support in every crazy adventure I come up with;

To my daughters, Ella and Aubrey, who have shown me what it's all for: Thank you.

CONTENTS

INTRODUCTION

Congratulations! You've reached a significant milestone in your financial journey: *Two-Comma Wealth*. This term refers to a net worth of a million dollars or more in investable assets—a symbol of financial success achieved through hard work and smart decisions. It's a remarkable accomplishment that deserves recognition and celebration. Often seen as a marker of "complete success," two-comma wealth is the stuff dreams are made of and even the inspiration for game shows. After all, who *doesn't* want to be a millionaire? You've worked hard, made strategic choices, and now stand at the threshold of a new chapter in your financial journey. Whether you're revisiting your approach, realizing the need for a new direction, or adjusting to a significant life event like a business sale, inheritance, retirement, or divorce, this moment calls for reflection. What got you here may not get you there—especially if "there" is still undefined. The path forward requires more than financial knowledge; it calls for the confidence, vision, and clarity to navigate your wealth with a fresh approach.

Most financial advisory books focus on how to accumulate wealth, but they rarely address the unique challenges that arise once you've reached a substantial level of prosperity. This book fills that gap by focusing on individuals and families managing $1 million–$30 million in investable assets. Positioned between basic personal finance guidance and the nuanced strategies tailored for those of ultra-high net worth—approaches that apply to only a select few—this growing demographic often requires tailored, practical advice. With millions of households achieving two-comma wealth through rising home values, equity compensation, entrepreneurial success, and diligent investment strategies, the need for targeted financial guidance has never been greater.

Despite their financial success, individuals in this category often grapple with concerns that are surprisingly similar to those of many American households: navigating economic uncertainty, managing taxes, addressing rising health-care costs, and planning for the future. While they have achieved a significant milestone, their worries frequently center on providing for their families, securing their financial well-being, and making informed decisions in an increasingly complex world. For many, wealth is a relative concept, after all. Those with two-comma wealth often don't perceive themselves as "rich" but as everyday individuals striving to preserve and grow their hard-earned nest eggs while avoiding potential financial missteps.

I understand these concerns deeply, not only through my work but also through my own family's journey. My father's story as an immigrant from a small Greek farm town with only a fourth-grade education taught me the value of resilience and hard work. I can still remember the scent of restaurant kitchens on his clothes as he came home late, driven by his dream of a brighter future for our family. Over time, my family transitioned from humble beginnings to two-comma wealth—a journey familiar to many first-generation millionaires. This personal journey shaped my understanding of the opportunities and challenges that come with wealth, inspiring me to dedicate my career to helping others navigate similar paths. Balancing immediate needs with long-term goals, overcoming financial uncertainty, and managing wealth wisely can make a profound difference. Effective wealth management ensures that wealth is preserved, grows strategically, and is used purposefully—not squandered or lost to excessive taxes or unnecessary market risks.

These principles resonate deeply with many of my clients, offering opportunities to create meaningful legacies while addressing everyday challenges. My parents instilled in me the value of hard work, resilience, and making sound financial decisions—principles that continue to shape my approach to advising clients today. As I pursued my education and entered the world of finance, I was drawn to the complexities of managing substantial wealth and the significant impact it can have on individuals and families. To better serve this demographic, I deliberately sought out advanced credentials tailored to their unique needs, such as the CERTIFIED FINANCIAL PLANNER™ (CFP®), Certified Exit Planning Advisor® (CEPA®), and Certified Private Wealth Advisor® (CPWA®) designations. These qualifications have allowed me to channel my expertise into guiding clients through the intricate challenges of wealth management in ways that make a meaningful difference for them and their families.

Specializing in investment, tax, and estate strategies, I've had the privilege of helping hundreds of families navigate their unique financial journeys, using many of the strategies outlined in *Two-Comma Wealth*. Through these experiences, I've gained invaluable insight into the diverse challenges and opportunities wealth can bring. My hope is that this book provides you with valuable insights to support your own path, equipping you to preserve, grow, and use your wealth with purpose. In fact, the principles and strategies in this book are summarized in what I call SWIM: Stefanou Wealth and Investment Management. SWIM offers a structured approach to help you navigate the complexities of wealth with clarity and confidence, ensuring you can achieve your goals while building a meaningful legacy.

Over the years, I have worked with individuals and families from all walks of life, each with unique circumstances and aspirations. These experiences have allowed me the perspective to live, in a sense, hundreds of different lives and navigate thousands of unique scenarios. As an experienced practitioner with over fifteen years of hands-on expertise—and recognized as a Forbes-ranked top advisor for the last two consecutive years—I bring these lived experiences to life in this book. This is not a theoretical guide written by a professor; it is a practical road map authored by someone who has witnessed firsthand what works and what doesn't. By leveraging the collective wisdom gained from guiding so many, I aim to provide you with the tools and strategies to confidently navigate this phase of your financial journey and achieve your goals.

In today's information-saturated world, it's easy to feel lost amidst conflicting advice from financial pundits, podcasters, and even well-meaning friends and family. This book aims to cut through the noise, providing a clear, actionable road map based on real-world client experiences. Managing substantial wealth brings unique responsibilities. It's not just about accumulation; it's about balancing everyday challenges with strategic decisions to ensure a meaningful life and lasting legacy. We'll explore the following:

- Investment strategies to help preserve and grow your wealth even through volatile markets
- Tax considerations to optimize your financial outcomes and avoid common mistakes hidden throughout the over eighty thousand pages of the tax code and IRS regulations and guidance
- Estate planning intricacies to protect and distribute your assets according to your wishes

While these topics may seem daunting, I aim to demystify them and offer actionable strategies you can confidently implement. Financial education is empowering, and with the right knowledge and tools, you'll be well-prepared to navigate the challenges and opportunities of two-comma wealth.

Whether you're new to this level of wealth or have been managing it for some time, this book is designed for you. I understand that financial matters can feel intimidating, but with proper guidance, you can successfully navigate this phase of your financial journey. By the end of this book, you'll have gained not only financial knowledge but also the peace of mind that comes from making informed decisions. Together, we'll break down complex financial concepts into clear, actionable steps toward achieving your goals.

This book is designed to provide practical strategies to maximize your wealth, minimize tax burdens, and create a lasting legacy—all while keeping the guidance relatable and actionable. Welcome to *Two-Comma Wealth: Investment, Tax, and Estate Strategies to Consider When Your Net Worth Exceeds a Million Dollars*. As both a financial expert and a self-proclaimed dad-joke expert (just ask my teenage daughters), I'd say that in a world drowning in investment advice, this book is really a masterclass in learning how to SWIM: Stefanou Wealth and Investment Management.

Each chapter concludes with SWIM Lessons—practical, actionable takeaways to guide your journey. These lessons will help you refine your financial strategies, from optimizing investments to managing tax burdens with thoughtful timing. As you read, take a moment to reflect on these lessons, consider how they apply to your situation, and start implementing them step by step. Now, let's dive in together!

CHAPTER ONE

The Path to Two-Comma Wealth

Success is the sum of small efforts,

repeated day in and day out.

—ROBERT COLLIER

My father, trapped in the cycle of poverty in his hometown in Greece, made a daring decision that would change the course of his life. He decided to jump ship—not *quite* literally. You see, at seventeen, he begged his father to sign the necessary paperwork to allow him to work in the Greek shipping industry and travel the world. One fateful day, while the ship was ported in America, he walked down the gangplank into Philadelphia and never went back. With his monthly stipend of only $300 in his pocket and an extra pair of underwear (which, as we can all acknowledge, is rather important), he hitched a ride to New Jersey, ready to embark on a new chapter.

After arriving in New Jersey, he wasted no time finding work. Determination fueled him as he secured a job as a line cook in a bustling restaurant. My father was a true penny-pincher, saving every dollar he could manage while working seven days a week, eating where he worked, and living in the small apartment directly above the restaurant to cut expenses. He sent money back home to his family whenever possible. His goal was to expand his career opportunities and move from Mesaia Milia, the small tobacco crop town of 293 people where he grew up, to the city of Katerini, Greece, where work could be found outside of farm life, but only if you had the means to live there. That was the dream, and coming to America was a brief means to that end.

Life took an unexpected turn when he met my mother, and they decided to start a family together. As the number of mouths to feed grew, so did the costs. The soaring housing prices in New Jersey in the '80s only made the dream of being a homeowner and settling down more difficult. But my father was undeterred. He scraped together every penny he had saved to purchase a home. But the realtor he worked with said the $30k my mom and he had saved wouldn't be enough for a doghouse in the neighborhoods they were seeking. So, they moved to Florida, where (at that time) you could get a lot more house for your dollar, and their first venture into real estate began.

Growing up, I saw firsthand the sacrifices my father made. He was a man who smelled like the kitchens he worked tirelessly in, but he never complained. We took a trip each year to visit family in either New Jersey or Greece, and because he didn't have a job with benefits or official PTO, sometimes he came back to find that the handshake deal he had made with the owner before he left was not honored, and he had been replaced by another cook. My dad, with only a fourth-grade education and not many job prospects, always reminded me of the educational and professional opportunities provided to me by this country that he wasn't afforded. Like so many immigrants before him, he was constantly working, driven by a relentless pursuit of providing for his family—the American dream. He lived by the simple principle of living on even less than the small amount he earned, diligently saving what he could, and though we never had excess, we were never left without the basics in life. After the second time my dad came back from our annual family trip to be greeted with no job and no recourse against the lies he had been told, he decided to create a secondary income source. He purchased an investment property, a home that had burned down. He learned how to fix it up and rent it out. I helped with things he delegated to me, like filing the taxes and writing the rental agreements. By the third time he returned from vacation without a job, he had three properties and would never return to working for someone else again. As time passed, he began acquiring more and more properties. Slowly but surely, he was building his very own empire.

Years later, my father achieved what I affectionately call two-comma wealth. His net worth hit the seven-figure mark, adding that second comma that comes with crossing the million-dollar milestone and beyond. But here's the funny part: he didn't even realize it. His penny-pinching ways were so ingrained that the idea of being a millionaire seemed far-fetched. He was trying to be financially secure and make his way. It took a chance encounter with his realtor to bring this realization to light.

One ordinary day, my father walked into the real estate office, unaware of the financial milestone he had reached. He came to his realtor with one of his infamously low-ball offers on a property he had found because, after all, as he would often say, "You never know if you don't ask!"

That's when his realtor, with a knowing smile, casually dropped the bombshell: "You know you are a millionaire, right?" At first, my father's face looked quizzical, as if he couldn't quite comprehend what he was hearing. The realtor reiterated, "You have over a million dollars in assets. You are a millionaire."

Then, a slow realization dawned on my father, and he replied with surprise and humility, "Well, I guess I am."

> *My father achieved what I affectionately call two-comma wealth. His net worth hit the seven-figure mark, adding that second comma that comes with crossing the million-dollar milestone and beyond.*

The Money Mindsets

In my line of work, I frequently encounter individuals who, for lack of a better phrase, started from the bottom. These are folks who, like my dad, began their financial journeys with a scarcity mindset, and even now, as they find themselves in the realm of two-comma wealth, they don't identify as millionaires and don't consider themselves wealthy. Many remain trapped in that scarcity mindset. It's a curious phenomenon—one that profoundly influences their financial decisions and limits their willingness to fully embrace the opportunities their wealth affords.

Many remain trapped

in that scarcity mindset.

This scarcity mindset has a far-reaching impact. It affects the risks they're willing to take, the subsidies they're hesitant to relinquish, and the budgets they're comfortable with. Their past struggles and experiences have left a lasting imprint on their financial outlook, deeply influencing their views on money and abundance. This phenomenon is not uncommon among those who have newly acquired wealth. As James Grubman, PhD, and Dennis Jaffe, PhD, note in their paper "Immigrants and Natives to Wealth: Understanding Clients Based on Their Wealth Origins":

> Those who acquire wealth through the development and sale of a business typically have a more fully formed sense of self before coming to wealth. They carry their 'old country' values inside them as they experience transition and transformation. They may, for example, worry about becoming the very stereotype of the rich as spoiled, self-absorbed, shallow, and snobbish.[1]

Don't get me wrong. As a CERTIFIED FINANCIAL PLANNER™ professional, I'm the first to tell someone if they are overspending, but often, people fail to realize they are indeed wealthy and that breaking free from this scarcity mindset is crucial if we are to unlock the full potential of wealth and create a life of not just financial abundance, but one of fulfillment.

Contrary to popular belief, millionaires aren't solely the product of generational wealth, born into privilege. A staggering 80 percent of millionaires in the United States are newcomers to wealth, according to Grubman and Jaffe. They are individuals who have built something from the ground up, diligently saved for years, built and sold a business successfully, or simply managed their money wisely. It's a truth that echoes the sentiment of *The Millionaire Next Door*, where you might encounter someone on the street who possesses considerable wealth, yet you'd be completely unaware of it. And that's perfectly all right. But it's time we reframed the narrative surrounding two-comma wealth.

A staggering 80 percent of millionaires in the United States are newcomers to wealth, according to Grubman and Jaffe.

The famous $75,000 study conducted by Princeton researchers in 2010 found that higher incomes do indeed lead to greater happiness, but only up to a certain threshold of around $75,000 per year.[2] Beyond that point, further increases in income had diminishing returns on subjective well-being. This aligns with the principles of Maslow's hierarchy of needs, which suggests that once physiological and safety needs are met, people are then driven by a desire for love/belonging, esteem, and, ultimately, self-actualization.[3]

For those fortunate enough to have accumulated two-comma wealth, the opportunity to fulfill the higher-order needs on Maslow's pyramid becomes a very real possibility. No longer constrained by financial concerns around basic survival, those with significant wealth can focus on cultivating meaningful relationships, pursuing personal growth and creative endeavors, and leaving a lasting positive impact on the world.

However, simply having the resources is not enough. In my work, I've found that many two-comma wealth individuals still struggle to translate their wealth into true, lasting happiness. This is where the guidance of an experienced advisor can be invaluable.

By taking the time to deeply understand a client's values, aspirations, and "bucket list" of life goals, a trusted advisor can help them create a financial plan that is aligned with their unique path to self-actualization.

By taking the time to deeply understand a client's values, aspirations, and "bucket list" of life goals, a trusted advisor can help them create a financial plan that is aligned with their unique path to self-actualization.

For instance, I recently worked with a client who had a sizable certificate of deposit (CD) coming due. When I asked how she might use the funds, she initially said she didn't think she'd ever need the money. She and her husband were already living comfortably on their Social Security and pension income and thought they'd simply add it to their investment accounts. Their portfolio was already well into two-comma territory, and they had no plans to spend it all. Many advisors might have accepted this at face value and moved on, but I decided to dig a bit deeper.

I asked the client, "If you *had* to spend the money, what would you spend it on?" The couple looked at each other, surprised—they had never truly considered that question. After a moment, the client shared that her niece had an upcoming destination wedding in Mexico. They had been hesitant to attend due to the expense, but with the matured CD funds, they could easily afford to celebrate this special occasion.

Additionally, they could upgrade to business class flights to make the travel more enjoyable without impacting their financial security. We worked together to make it happen. During this conversation, they also revealed other dreams they had never expressed before, including a transcontinental train trip that one spouse had secretly wished for. By exploring these possibilities, we turned a simple financial decision into a plan filled with purpose and joy.

It's not just about the numbers in your bank account; it's about using your wealth to align with your values and live your purpose.

This story highlights an important truth: wealth alone does not bring fulfillment. It's not just about the numbers in your bank account; it's about using your wealth to align with your values and live your purpose. The key is finding balance—enjoying the fruits of your hard work while making thoughtful decisions to secure your future. As the saying goes, "You never see a U-Haul following a hearse." Your wealth should not merely accumulate; it should serve a meaningful purpose that enriches your life and the lives of those you care about.

By understanding both sides of the spectrum—the individuals who remain trapped in scarcity despite their wealth and those who squander their riches—we can find the middle ground. It is within that balance that true financial freedom and fulfillment reside.

Tolerance for Risk

When it comes to investing, risk is always part of the equation. I frequently work with clients who are very cautious when it comes to taking risks with their money. And while it's important to manage and mitigate risk, it's also essential to recognize that sometimes taking

While it's important to manage and mitigate risk, it's also essential to recognize that sometimes taking a measure of calculated risk is often necessary to reach your financial goals and can lead to significant returns.

a measure of calculated risk is often necessary to reach your financial goals and can lead to significant returns. I would say the majority of people who I sit down with tell me they are not big risk-takers and that they want a conservative approach. This is due to the powerful emotional bias called loss aversion. Some psychological studies have shown that the pain of loss is twice as powerful as the joy of gains.

The irony here is that most people who are first-generation millionaires took risks to get there. They took a risk to start their business—perhaps bootstrapping it and barely making ends meet—or perhaps they built a real estate empire leveraging properties with mortgages, or they were executives that held highly concentrated stock positions, or they diligently invested into stock mutual funds or ETFs in their 401(k)s over time. Each of those has risks, but interestingly, our perception of risk is not uniform. We don't view the business we own as risky, we don't view our company stock as risky, we don't view our investment properties as risky, and for some reason (at least while the market is up), we may not view our 401(k)s as risky. When we no longer associate those assets with a business or our employment, we view it as something unknown and, therefore, somehow assume it is unsafe.

I assure you, though, that all these assets carry risks, even if we don't always recognize them. Let's focus on owning real estate as an example, since it's often where I see the most disconnect. Real estate is inherently risky, though we tend to overlook this. Consider what happened during the financial crisis of 2008. In many ways, owning investment property can pose greater risks than other investments.

When was the last time a mutual fund, ETF, or publicly traded stock you owned called you to fix a plumbing issue, threatened to sue you over a slip-and-fall accident, or required you to pay property taxes or the deductible on a property insurance claim? These are risks unique to real estate ownership, yet many perceive it as safer simply because it feels tangible and within their control. This perception can lead to a false sense of security while the true time and effort required to manage properties are often underestimated. Social media may glorify real estate as "mailbox money," but in reality, it's running a business—one that comes with its own challenges and risks. We'll delve further into the parallels between real estate investing and business risks in chapter 8, where we explore these topics in greater detail.

So why do so many people view investment property as less risky than the stock market? It's largely because they feel they can influence the outcome of their success and because real estate is something they can see and touch—it feels familiar and understandable. But if we were to assign a value to the time and effort it takes to manage the property, many would be surprised at the income disparity. The truth is people fear what they don't understand. When clients come to my office and describe themselves as conservative investors, what they are often expressing is a fear of the unknown. They need clarity and understanding about what they're investing in. In most cases, they are comfortable with certain levels of risk because, more often than not, that's exactly how they accumulated their wealth in the first place—it was through risks they understood. I will do my very best to help you understand the world of investing with two-comma wealth and further conquer this fear in chapter 4 of this book.

Just like real estate, the stock market carries significant risks— but unlike tangible assets, its risks often feel harder to understand, leading to common missteps by investors. For instance, we all know the adage that we should buy low and sell high, but more often than not, the average investor does the complete opposite. DALBAR, a company that has tracked the average investor returns compared to the market averages for forty years, has conducted many studies about this phenomenon. While reviewing DALBAR's studies, I think CNBC identified the problem quite well:

> Since 1988, the stock market's average return has been 10% per year. But stock fund investors have earned only 4.1% per year, according to DALBAR's Quantitative Analysis of Investor Behavior. So, why are investors missing out on 60% of the market's profits? Because your brain gets in the way. Survival instincts have evolved into 'behavior biases' that cause us to make bad financial and investment decisions. Understanding them can help you avoid costly mistakes.[4]

After all, if we live in a world where a well-diversified portfolio of quality companies can no longer find a way to make money and grow in value, then we likely have bigger fish to fry!

One way I help clients avoid behavioral bias is by being up front and honest with them about how the market works. During every financial cycle, there are ups and downs. And each and every downturn has been followed by a recovery and, eventually, a new all-time high. That will continue to be the case until it isn't, and if it is no longer the case, then we have far more to worry about than the stock market at that point. After all, if we live in a world where a well-diversified portfolio of quality companies can no longer find a way to make money and grow in value, then we likely have bigger fish to fry! (Like investing in an underground shelter, satellite phones, and plenty of dry goods.)

Money is not just about the numbers on a statement, though; it's also tied to the hard work and effort you put into earning it. We all have dreams and aspirations that our money represents, and when we perceive those dreams and aspirations being threatened, it's natural to feel a sense of panic. This emotional connection to our money can make us risk-averse, as we fear losing what we've worked so hard to achieve. When you've put in sweat equity to earn your money, it becomes deeply intertwined with your work ethic, and that can make you more cautious about taking risks.

When you've put in sweat equity to earn your money, it becomes deeply intertwined with your work ethic, and that can make you more cautious about taking risks.

While being risk-averse is understandable, it's also essential to recognize that growth and opportunity often come with a degree of risk, and it is likely a higher degree of risk that got you to two-comma wealth to begin with! I always find it so interesting that those same clients who consider themselves conservative will "bet the farm" on an industry they are familiar with. Whether that is the concentrated stock they have held onto, the business they own, or the real estate portfolio they have been involved in, they will easily lack diversification and get caught up in those investments because they *understand* them. Knowledge is power, especially when it comes to investing. Warren Buffet made billions by investing in companies he knew, understood, and used himself, so it's natural and beneficial to do the same. But if we take "the market" out of the market and break down investments so we truly understand what we are getting into, we don't have to work *for* our money. Our money can begin to work *for* us, which is something we will cover in greater detail later in this book. By carefully assessing and managing that risk, you can increase your chances of achieving greater financial returns. It's about finding that sweet spot where you're comfortable with the level of risk you're taking while still pursuing your financial goals.

I encourage you to ask yourself:

What keeps you up at night? What are your biggest hopes
and fears when it comes to your next phase in life?

By understanding your unique tolerance for risk, you can work to craft a plan that allows you to pursue your passions while also providing the stability and security you need to thrive in whatever life stage you are in.

Behavioral Finance: The Key to Better Decisions

Your financial mindset profoundly influences how you approach wealth, shaping decisions about risk, savings, and growth. While the earlier story of my father's journey highlights the importance of hard work and discipline, maintaining and growing wealth—especially at the two-comma level—requires more than just grit. It demands a clear understanding of how our emotions and biases can inadvertently steer us off course.

Earlier, we referenced findings from a past DALBAR study that revealed the significant gap between the returns of the average investor and broader market indices. A more recent study, the *2023 DALBAR Quantitative Analysis of Investor Behavior (QAIB)*,[5] reaffirms these findings, highlighting how emotional biases remain a primary reason investors underperform. Over the past twenty years, the average equity mutual fund investor earned an annualized return of just 6.81 percent, compared to the S&P 500 Index's 9.65 percent. This underperformance wasn't due to a lack of investment options but was largely the result of emotional mistakes—panic selling during downturns or chasing hot stocks during rallies.

What keeps you up at night? What are your biggest hopes and fears when it comes to your next phase in life?

For a $1 million portfolio, the difference between these returns is striking. At 6.81 percent, the portfolio grows to $3.73 million over twenty years. In contrast, staying invested at the S&P 500's return of 9.65 percent grows the same portfolio to $6.31 million—a $2.58 million shortfall for the average investor. Imagine spending twenty years watching your portfolio grow to $3.73 million, only to find out your neighbor, with the same $1 million ended up with $6.31 million simply by staying the course and avoiding emotional decisions. It's like training for a marathon only to find out your friend skipped the run, took a shortcut, and still ended up with the gold medal while you settled for the bronze.

At the two-comma wealth level, investing is no longer just a casual hobby or a personal milestone like running a marathon. Instead, it represents a pivotal responsibility with lasting consequences for your financial future and the legacy you aim to build. Investing is no longer about casual experiments or chasing trends; it's about securing a future, protecting what you've built, and ensuring it grows wisely. It's also not completely passive or something to be ignored—missteps carry significant consequences, and going it alone without a professional advisor is often a risk too great to bear. Even Vanguard®, a company renowned for its support of DIY investors, has acknowledged the challenges individual investors face. Their *Advisor's Alpha®* study quantifies how skilled advisors can enhance client outcomes by adding up to 3 percent in net annual returns through strategies like behavioral coaching, tax optimization, and cost-effective portfolio management.[6]

This acknowledgment serves as a reminder that even the most self-directed investors can benefit from professional guidance, especially at two-comma wealth where decisions carry greater stakes. These three areas—*behavioral coaching, tax strategies,* and *cost-effective portfolio management and rebalancing*—are critical components of advisor-added value, and this book will explore each. As we proceed, I'll show how these strategies can be applied to your unique circumstances, offering insights on how to maximize their benefits.

Recognizing what sets a truly exceptional financial advisor apart involves understanding their ability to combine technical expertise with genuine empathy and personalized care.

When I sit down with clients, I don't just see them as clients. I imagine myself as a fly on the wall, watching as my children, spouse, sibling, or parent meet with an advisor. What would I want that advisor to address? What critical topics might they overlook? What strategies would ensure my loved ones' financial well-being? This perspective drives me to focus on what truly matters—not just for today but for their long-term security and success.

This mindset compels me to dig deeper, ensuring that no essential aspect of financial planning is missed. It's not about checking boxes or offering generic advice—it's about tailoring strategies to the unique circumstances of each family, just as I would for my own. The right advisor doesn't stop at reviewing financial statements; they should analyze tax returns, family goals, and personal dynamics. These foundational steps are just the beginning. True value comes from crafting a living, evolving partnership that adapts to life's changes. Vanguard's Advisor's Alpha® study highlights this dynamic approach—where strategies like behavioral coaching, tax optimization, and portfolio management not only improve returns but also provide peace of mind through a clear and ongoing plan.

I had a personal reminder of this value when my wife, Kristin, asked me to prepare a plan for her in case I passed away—a sobering thought. I wrote her a detailed email outlining where to find our accounts, life insurance policies, and a breakdown of my investment methodology and selection process. I thought I had covered everything. But when we reviewed it, she asked, "Who do I go to see to get this all done?" At first, I was taken aback—I was an expert in this field and had outlined every step. I also knew our situation better than anyone. Why would she need to hire a professional? Then she explained: without me, the sheer detail of it all was overwhelming.

She wouldn't have the expertise, interest, or confidence to handle it alone. She wanted to feel safe and reassured about the decisions she'd need to make—or avoid—on her own. Interestingly, without ever reading a word of the Vanguard Advisor's Alpha® study, she had identified its most important component: the value of behavioral guidance.

This experience prompted me to take a crucial step—not just for Kristin but for all my clients. I hired an associate financial advisor, someone I could partner with to learn my methods and serve as a continuity plan in case of my unexpected demise. Succession planning is an essential part of ensuring long-term security and confidence for clients, and it's a key factor to consider when selecting a financial advisor. It's not just about having a plan for the investments; it's about having a plan for the advisor too.

That moment underscored an essential truth: the value of a skilled advisor isn't just in providing information but in delivering a sense of security and partnership. It's about offering clarity during life's complexities and confidence during uncertain times.

This experience reinforces a fundamental principle: financial planning isn't just about managing numbers—it's about managing lives, expectations, and emotions. By understanding your complete financial landscape—your investments, taxes, estate plan, family dynamics, and personal goals—and pairing that understanding with disciplined, strategic guidance, an advisor can turn complexity into clarity. Strategies like behavioral coaching, tax optimization, and portfolio management bring measurable value to your financial future while also providing peace of mind. Let's explore how such a financial advisory relationship can make a meaningful difference for you.

To illustrate the impact on the average investor, as outlined in the Quantitative Analysis of Investor Behavior (QAIB) study and Vanguard's Advisor's Alpha® framework, let's revisit a $1 million portfolio—this time incorporating the potential benefits of expert guidance.

STRATEGY APPLIED	NET ANNUAL RETURN	PORTFOLIO VALUE AFTER 20 YEARS	INCREASED VALUE OVER AVERAGE INVESTOR
Average Investor (QAIB Study)	6.81%	$3,734,550	—
With Behavioral Coaching (+1.5%)	8.31%	$4,935,954	+$1,201,404
With Tax Strategies (+1.2%)	9.51%	$6,152,839	+$2,418,289
With Portfolio Management (+0.45%)	9.96%	$6,678,741	+$2,944,191

These figures, based on findings from the 2023 DALBAR QAIB and 2022 Vanguard Advisor's Alpha® studies, demonstrate the transformational potential of professional advice. For example, by incorporating strategies like behavioral coaching, the portfolio potential grows by an additional $1.2 million over twenty years. Adding tax strategies increases the portfolio's total potential by more than $2.4 million compared to the average investor. And with the full suite of strategies—including portfolio management—the total potential value climbs to nearly $6.7 million, an increase of $2.9 million over the baseline.

These outcomes depend on the advisor's expertise and the unique needs of each client, making the selection of the right advisor and their team a critical decision—a topic we'll explore further later in the book.

At the heart of all this is a reminder: managing two-comma wealth isn't about competing with the S&P 500 Index or chasing arbitrary benchmarks. Instead, it's about focusing on your *personal benchmark*—the specific returns and strategies needed to optimize your plan to meet your goals and sustain your financial well-being. Whether it's funding your retirement, creating a legacy, or simply enjoying the fruits of your labor, aligning your financial decisions with what truly matters to you is the key to success. With this foundation in mind, let's turn our attention to defining and prioritizing those goals—ensuring they reflect your unique mindset and financial priorities while paving the way for long-term fulfillment.

Level-Setting Around Goals

Financial goals must be aligned with your risk tolerance and mindset. Let's explore some key considerations and strategies to ensure your goals are realistic, achievable, and in line with your financial well-being.

UNLIMITED RISK TOLERANCE ON THE UPSIDE: It's natural to get excited about the potential for high investment returns and dream of unlimited financial success. People love to swing for the fences and do so often in things like the state lottery. Most understand the statistics are not in their favor, and the money spent is likely just being thrown away, but that incredibly small chance of exponential returns makes it worth the likely loss. However, a few bucks tossed out in a lottery ticket isn't viewed the same way as a more sizable investment is. When it comes to your two-comma wealth nest egg, it's often equally as important to protect yourself from large potential losses as it is to seek out large potential gains. Finding a balance between growth and risk management is essential for long-term financial stability. For example, imagine you have $1,000,000 invested. If you experience a 50 percent loss, you would be left with $500,000. To get back to your original $1,000,000, you can't just achieve a 50 percent return. You would need a 100 percent return—a doubling of your remaining $500,000 to break even. On the other hand, a 20 percent loss would leave you with $800,000, requiring only a 25 percent return to recover your initial investment. And a 10 percent loss could be recouped with just over an 11 percent gain.

When it comes to your two-comma wealth nest egg, it's often equally as important to protect yourself from large potential losses as it is to seek out large potential gains.

This asymmetry is why everyone's instinct is to seek outsized 100 percent returns, though they may overlook the risk of corresponding 50 percent drops that come with such investments. If you reframe the scenario by increasing the amount invested and emphasizing the potential loss first, most people's risk tolerance shifts noticeably. A more balanced approach, one that mitigates those extreme peaks and valleys, can be the wiser path to long-term financial stability and well-being. The key to investing with and staying in two-comma wealth, like golf, isn't all about hitting long drives; it's about staying in play and making consistently good shots, not occasionally great shots.

A more balanced approach, one that mitigates those extreme peaks and valleys, can be the wiser path to long-term financial stability and well-being.

Likewise, with significant wealth, many find that aiming for consistently good returns feels more secure than chasing the occasional great one, given the large loss potential. In fact, two-comma wealth can break that conventional mindset—by balancing risk with reward, investors can avoid having to swing for the fences. Many with two-comma wealth appreciate that they no longer face an all-or-nothing scenario; steady, consistent gains can win the game when it comes to reaching your financial goals. This doesn't mean you should bunt with every at-bat, as failing to get on base might leave you vulnerable to losing money to inflation and not having enough to meet your long term goals at the bottom of the ninth inning; but with a long-term mindset focused on your goals, the basics of a high-quality, well-diversified portfolio can ultimately be your winning strategy and reduce anxiety along the way.

THE INFLUENCE OF MINDSET ON GOAL SETTING: Your mindset plays a significant role in how you set your financial goals. Take a moment to reflect on your beliefs, values, and attitudes toward money. Consider your past experiences and any fears or limiting beliefs that might hinder your progress. Understanding your mindset will help you set goals that are meaningful, realistic, and aligned with your values.

When working with clients, I often use three columns to categorize their financial goals: needs, wants, and wishes.

> *Needs:* These are essential goals for your well-being and financial security. This includes having your investments cover your basic monthly and nonrecurring but anticipated expenses. This would include food, housing, basic repairs, transportation costs, utilities and health-care premiums, and copays. But it also includes taking care of some blind spots in this goal, for instance, building an emergency fund to cover unexpected expenses, paying off high-interest debt to reduce financial stress, or securing adequate insurance coverage for protection. Meeting these needs should be your top priority when setting goals.

> *Wants:* Wants are important goals that may not be immediate necessities but hold significance in your life. Examples could include remodeling your home, funding a child's education to invest in their future opportunities, or taking a dream vacation to create lasting memories. Prioritizing these goals will depend on your unique circumstances and financial capacity.

> *Wishes:* Wishes represent aspirational and long-term goals that require more time and resources to achieve. Examples

could include early retirement, buying a second home, paying for your granddaughter's college or your daughter's wedding, starting your own business to pursue your passion, or engaging in philanthropic endeavors to make a positive impact. While wishes may require more effort and planning, they can serve as a source of inspiration and motivation for your financial journey. And no one is here to judge you on your wants or wishes. The reality is that one person's wants may be another person's wishes, and vice versa.

By categorizing your goals into these three columns, you gain clarity on what truly matters to you and can allocate your resources accordingly. It allows you to prioritize your needs, consider your wants, and work toward fulfilling your wishes in a balanced manner.

Money is emotional, and it's important to spend it on the things that bring you joy. For example, my father, despite being frugal with his finances, values dining out at restaurants. This is likely because he spent much of his life as a line cook and now wants to enjoy the fruits of someone else's labor, something he views as a part of his regular budget and, therefore, a *need*. He *wants* to do a family cruise every year or two, where he gathers my sister, me, and our families to join in. And his *wish* was to build a home in the city of Katerini, Greece, that he and my mother could visit several times a year. It all comes down to personal perspective—what is important to you and how you want to spend your wealth. It's not about frivolous spending but rather planned budgeting and meaningfully allocating your resources accordingly. Time is something we can't get back, and both the adages "Time is money" and "Money is time" hold

> *The reality is that one person's wants may be another person's wishes, and vice versa.*

true. It's about balancing a healthy portfolio that aligns with your values and priorities. Wealth is a state of mind. Money is but a tool to realize it.

SWIM Lessons

At the end of each chapter, you'll find something I like to call SWIM Lessons—Stefanou Wealth and Investment Management Lessons. Just like learning to swim helps you navigate the water with confidence, these lessons are designed to help you swim through the often murky waters of personal finance. I know it can feel overwhelming at times, with waves of information coming at you from all directions. The idea here is to give you clear, actionable steps so you no longer feel like you're struggling to stay afloat.

There's also a deeper, personal connection to this concept. My father, despite coming from a country famous for its beaches and arriving in America by ship, never learned how to swim. So, these SWIM Lessons are not only practical tools to help you avoid feeling overwhelmed, but they're also a tribute to his journey.

Each chapter will end with these SWIM Lesson summaries, along with questions to help you apply what you've learned. By the time you finish this book, my goal is that you'll feel empowered to dive confidently into your financial future with no fear of sinking—just steady progress toward your goals.

SWIM Lesson 1

SWIM Lesson:
Mindset Shapes Wealth

Remember that your mindset is the foundation of your financial decisions. A scarcity mindset can hold you back, even when you have wealth, while an abundance mindset allows you to embrace opportunities and align your wealth with your values.

ACTION STEP: Reflect on one belief about money that stems from your upbringing and write down how it has impacted your financial decisions today. Then consider one action you can take to reframe or challenge this belief.

> EXAMPLE
> - *Belief:* "I must save every penny because financial security is fragile."
> - *Reframe:* "I will build financial security by balancing saving with purposeful spending and investing in opportunities that align with my goals."

QUESTION: How has your mindset influenced your financial habits, and what steps can you take to shift from a scarcity to an abundance mindset?

_____

_____

_____

_____

SWIM Lesson:
Embrace Calculated Risks

Growth often requires stepping out of your comfort zone in measured ways. Avoid letting fear of the unknown stop you from making progress.

ACTION STEP: Identify one area where fear of risk has held you back financially. Take one small step to explore or address this fear, such as researching or discussing the potential risks and rewards with an advisor.

> EXAMPLE
> - *Perceived Risk:* "I feel safer with cash than investing in the market."
> - *Action:* "I'll meet with my advisor to discuss how a diversified portfolio can offer growth while managing risk."

QUESTION: What financial risks have you avoided, and how can better understanding those risks help you balance caution with opportunity?

_____

_____

_____

_____

_____

_____

_____

⊕ SWIM Lesson:
Align Goals with Your Values

Organizing your financial goals into categories—needs, wants, and wishes—helps you focus on what truly matters and prioritize your resources.

ACTION STEP: Write down one goal in each category (needs, wants, wishes). Take one small action in the next twenty-four hours to work toward a goal, such as reviewing your budget, starting a savings plan, or scheduling a financial review.

> EXAMPLE
> - *Need:* Build an emergency fund.
> - *Want:* Take a family vacation next year.
> - *Wish:* Retire early and travel the world.

QUESTION: How do your financial goals align with your values and long-term vision? Are you prioritizing your needs, while still making space for wants and wishes?

_____

_____

_____

_____

_____

_____

_____

_____

_____

_____

SWIM Lesson:
Behavioral Finance and Smart Decisions

Recognize how emotional biases can lead to poor financial decisions. Understanding these behaviors can help you stay the course and avoid costly mistakes.

ACTION STEP: Reflect on a recent emotionally driven financial decision (e.g., selling during a downturn or chasing a hot stock). Write down one action you could take next time to make a more rational choice.

EXAMPLE
- *Emotional Reaction:* Panic-sold during a market dip.
- *Action:* Review my financial plan during market volatility and focus on long-term goals instead of short-term fluctuations.

QUESTION: How can understanding your emotional triggers help you make smarter, more rational financial decisions?

_____

_____

_____

_____

_____

_____

_____

_____

_____

⊕ SWIM Lesson:
Build a Financial Compass and Continuity Plan

Your wealth plan should guide you like a compass, helping you make confident decisions even during uncertainty. It should also include a continuity strategy for your loved ones.

ACTION STEP: Review your financial plan to ensure it includes a continuity or succession plan for your family in case of unexpected circumstances. Identify areas where you may need to work with a professional to solidify this plan.

> EXAMPLE
> - *Plan Update:* "Confirm my advisor has a continuity strategy in place to support my family and manage my wealth in case of my absence."

QUESTION: Does your financial plan include a clear continuity strategy for your wealth and your family's long-term security?

_____

_____

_____

_____

_____

_____

_____

_____

_____

_____

CHAPTER TWO

Destination Unknown

Show where you spend your money and
I'll tell you what your priorities are.

—JAMES W. FRICK

I've never summited Mount Everest. And there are not many people in my circle who have. But I know that people plan for years to make the summit. They track their paths, prepare for the elevation changes, and ensure that they have enough gear and food to get to the top. They plan for the unexpected, whether it's storms, sickness, or above-average snowfall. Then they get to the top, and the whole trip, everything they have prepared for, culminates in a picture of them that they will put on their refrigerator and tell their kids about for years to come.

But the reality is that most fatal accidents that happen on Mount Everest occur on the way down.[7] It's the part that people don't plan as much. The "hype" is over, the goal has been reached, the pictures have been taken, and now, they're not 100 percent sure what to do. Going down the mountain can't be as difficult as getting up it, right? Some may think. And the lack of preparation on the descent is why accidents typically happen on the way down.

The same is true with millionaires. Everyone plans the first part: how to reach two-comma wealth. They watch YouTube videos and listen to podcasts. They read books. Perhaps they follow Dave Ramsey's baby steps, attend workshops and lectures, put money into a 401(k), and check all the boxes. Everyone wants to attain this lofty American dream; they want to reach the summit. But what do they do once they get there? What happens after years of planning and dreaming and saving and investing culminate in hitting your "number"? It's this question that prompted me to write this book. There are plenty of answers and opinions on how to achieve two-comma wealth, but not much out there for those who reach it in answering: Now what?

But what do they do once they get there? What happens after years of planning and dreaming and saving and investing culminate in hitting your "number"?

The real challenge often begins once you've reached the "summit" of your goals. Just like those Everest climbers, many people spend so much time and energy focused on the big milestone that they don't always have a clear plan for what comes next.

Reaching the top of the mountain is exhilarating, no doubt. But then reality sets in. The adrenaline fades and you're left to figure out how to safely navigate your way back down.

It's the same for people who've worked hard to build wealth and reach millionaire status. The initial drive to get there can be all-consuming. But once you've checked that box, you have to thoughtfully consider how to maintain, grow, and distribute your wealth over the long term. It's a whole new set of challenges that many aren't fully prepared for.

Just accumulating a million dollars doesn't automatically mean you'll know how to preserve and multiply that wealth. There's a skill set required to manage that kind of money responsibly. And if you don't have that know-how, you run the risk of making costly mistakes on the "descent"—losing it far quicker than you gained it. Money can be a lot like a good reputation: it takes a long time to build up a good amount, but just one bad decision can have you lose all that you've spent years building.

Money can be a lot like a good reputation: it takes a long time to build up a good amount, but just one bad decision can have you lose all that you've spent years building.

So, while climbing to the top is certainly worthy of celebration, the real test lies in what you do once you've reached the summit. That's where true mastery is achieved. The real challenge is in the journey to uncover the needs, wants, and wishes that will define what's next and determine how to achieve it as well. Much like Everest mountain climbers who hire a well-experienced sherpa to guide them and avoid the costly missteps of a wrong step along the way, my hope is this book serves as a guide to help you as you walk beyond the summit of two-comma wealth to realize and achieve whatever it is that is most important to you.

The Second Act

I work with a lot of clients who are nearing this pivotal moment, this transition into the next phase of their lives. They've spent years—maybe even decades—laser-focused on building up their net worth. And now that they've achieved that coveted two-comma status, they suddenly find themselves feeling a bit lost.

They have the financial freedom to do pretty much anything they want. But without that singular goal of wealth-building, they're not quite sure what to do with all this newfound time and flexibility. That's where I come in—to help them explore the endless possibilities for what I like to call their second act.

Maybe you want to quit the nine-to-five grind for good and never work another day in your life. Or maybe you enjoy the sense of purpose and human connection that comes from having a part-time gig—like my client who works as a greeter at a theme park or another who does so at the Home and Garden Center of Lowe's, just because they love interacting with people.

Perhaps your dream is to spend more quality time with loved ones, travel the world, or host elaborate dinner parties. Or maybe you want to pour your energy into a new business venture or find ways to give back and help others through volunteer work or philanthropy.

The point is, when you reach two-comma wealth, the future is truly yours to shape. It's not about someone else telling you how to spend your time and money. It's about identifying the things that will bring you genuine joy and fulfillment in this new chapter of your life.

Take my client who recently came into two-comma wealth while still living in Florida. During a period of self-discovery, she started taking trips to the mountains and fell head over heels for mountain biking. So for her second act, she decided to pull up stakes and move to Colorado, where she started her own mountain biking company.

Does she need the money? Absolutely not. But it brings her joy, which is really the whole point.

Another client had a lifelong dream of visiting every baseball stadium in the United States with his son. Well, with two-comma wealth under his belt, that dream became a reality. For another client, he loved the work we did for him and his family so much that he discovered his second act involved a complete career change—he decided to become a financial planner himself, and I was able to help him along that journey.

The point is, when you reach two-comma wealth, the future is truly yours to shape.

The common thread here is that, for these folks, reaching the summit of two-comma wealth wasn't the end of the story. It was just the beginning of a whole new adventure. They're using their resources to pursue passions, reconnect with loved ones, give back to their communities, and live even more fulfilling lives.

Money is just a tool.

Money is just a tool. And when you have two-comma wealth, your "second act" is all about figuring out how best to wield that tool in service of the life you truly want to live. It's not about someone else telling you how to spend your time and money. It's about taking the reins and shaping your future in a way that brings you joy, purpose, and genuine contentment.

The Obstacles

Take a moment, enjoy the view, and reflect well on the journey it took to get here and the blessing you have received to be at the vantage point you stand in as well. You've achieved a milestone that most of the world's population won't. However, you've also perhaps stumbled on a whole new set of challenges to navigate now that you are here.

A lot of those challenges stem from the fears and anxieties that can crop up when you suddenly find yourself in uncharted territory. I've encountered these concerns time and time again when meeting with my clients who've achieved this level of financial success.

A lot of those challenges

stem from the fears

and anxieties that

can crop up when you

suddenly find yourself

in uncharted territory.

Take my own parents, for instance. They're now well into two-comma wealth, but when I suggested they invest in a nice porch for their vacation home in the Poconos to make it more enjoyable and safer as they get older, my dad just couldn't stomach the idea. He feels guilty about spending the money, even though he can easily afford it. The penny-pinching ways that got him to two-comma wealth now have become a stumbling block to him enjoying it. He loves the outdoors and the fresh mountain air, and an open-air porch would undoubtedly bring him and my mother a lot of joy. But he continues to hold on to the old adage that if you watch the pennies, the dollars take care of themselves, and spent a year negotiating over the details of porch costs with different builders. I shared with him what I shared with you earlier in this book, that time is money too. We had a candid conversation about the reality that there is only so much time we have left in this world. We talked about how a year of negotiating over a few hundred or even a few thousand dollars was costing him lifetime enjoyment. For my dad, there was a mental block there. It was a fear of embracing and utilizing wealth because he felt like he needed permission to spend or else he was squandering money. I'm happy to report, after that conversation and some helpful piling on by my sister, they have their porch and enjoy every moment spent on it.

For others, I think a big part of their fear and anxiety comes down to identity, especially when transitioning out of the workforce. When we meet new people, the first two questions are almost always "What's your name?" and "What do you do for work?" And for those who've attained this level of wealth postretirement or business exit, the idea of not having that ready-made work identity can be really unsettling. They may wonder, "What am I going to do all day if I'm not running my business or climbing the corporate ladder?"

The idea of not having that ready-made work identity can be really unsettling.

And then there are the fears around longevity and legacy: Will the money last? What if I suffer investment losses? How do I ensure my heirs are taken care of? Not to mention the anxieties around health-care costs and nursing home expenses that can upend even the most carefully laid financial plans.

It's a lot to grapple with, no doubt. But you need to face those fears head-on, do an honest self-assessment, and figure out a plan to move forward. Because having two-comma wealth means you've got the resources to do so much good—for yourself, your loved ones, and your community. But you've got to be willing to embrace it and not let the anxiety hold you back. One thing that helps is to do the math and get yourself in the right mindset by realizing how to give yourself permission to spend. For now, let's walk through some basic principles you can apply to understand a range of spending to formulate a comfortable income strategy to draw from your two-comma wealth.

Determining a Budget

I'm not suggesting you use up all your wealth in one go. It's important to have a smart spending strategy, but don't shy away from enjoying what you've worked hard to earn. While we can't tackle everything on our "wishes" list right away, we can set up a plan to start checking things off, one by one.

For example, maybe you want to complete a kitchen renovation, go on a tour of Europe, and pay for your daughter's wedding. All of these things are feasible, but it would be unwise to try to do them all simultaneously. Instead, we can prioritize and phase them over time.

If you are still stuck in a scarcity mindset because you know what it was like to have little or nothing and don't want to go back, you need to give yourself permission to spend even incrementally. One way you can do so is by building your confidence that you do indeed have enough.

One approach I often make use of is the 4 percent rule. Here's how it works:

1. First, identify the amount of monthly income you need to cover your essential expenses—things like your mortgage, insurance, and basic living costs. Let's say that number is $10,000 per month above and beyond any pension or Social Security you may have coming in. That is the number you will need to draw from your portfolio to cover the income gap you have.

2. Multiply that $10,000 monthly by 12 to get your annual income needed—in this case, $120,000—then multiply that number by 25 to get $3,000,000. As long as $120,000 represents 4 percent or less of your overall portfolio, you can be fairly confident that you won't outlive your money caring for your basic expenses even when inflation is taken into account.

3. Now we can look at how to fund your "wants and wishes," with any margin you still have above that 25X figure. In this case, any excess above the $3 million can be used to fund any of those wants or wishes.

The "4 percent rule" is a widely used guideline in retirement planning, originating from the Trinity Study.

The "4 percent rule" is a widely used guideline in retirement planning, originating from the Trinity Study. This rule suggests withdrawing 4 percent of your initial retirement portfolio annually, adjusted for inflation, to sustain your savings over a thirty-year retirement period.[8]

For example, if you have $1 million saved, you could withdraw $40,000 in the first year, adjusting for inflation each subsequent year. The Trinity Study found that a balanced portfolio consisting of 50 percent stocks and 50 percent bonds historically supported this withdrawal rate with a high success rate over thirty years.

This is a good foundation for a brief discussion, but it isn't the end-all, be-all. It's important to consider that actual outcomes may vary based on market performance, inflation rates, and individual financial circumstances. That's where a full financial plan comes into play, but more on that later.

Be realistic about your needs, wants, and priorities at each stage of retirement. For instance, you may choose to withdraw more in your sixties while you have both the time and energy to be active (early retirement, or what I like to call the go-go years) and then scale back a bit in your seventies (your midretirement, or slow-go years) and eighties (your late retirement years, or no-go years). Now when you hit each of these and how much you spend will depend on your health and situation. Delaying Social Security can also help cushion your budget and cash flow later on, and we will discuss some of the tax advantages doing so may offer in chapters 5 and 6.

> *Be realistic about your needs, wants, and priorities at each stage of retirement.*

The important thing is having a plan. When working with clients, I often find it helpful to provide coaching around both sticking to a budget and also giving them that mental push (that "permission") to spend on the things that will truly enrich their lives and that, in doing so, things won't just be OK, they will be better for it.

We can start with a simple "back-of-the-napkin" calculation using the 4 percent rule, then refine the plan from there based on your unique goals and situation. At the end of the day, it is your money and your future, and a trusted advisor's job is to help you live the best life you possibly can while stewarding your wealth wisely.

Refining the 4 Percent Rule with Professional Planning

The 4 percent rule is a helpful guideline, but it's only a starting point. While it provides a simple way to estimate how much of your portfolio you can safely withdraw in retirement, real-life financial planning is far more nuanced. Variables like market volatility, unexpected expenses, changes in tax laws, and personal goals can all impact your portfolio's performance and sustainability.

To build confidence in your retirement plan, working with a financial planner is highly recommended. Professionals can tailor your plan using advanced tools such as *Monte Carlo analysis*, which goes beyond static calculations. Monte Carlo simulations project the likelihood of your plan's success by analyzing thousands of potential market scenarios, incorporating uncertainties like investment returns, inflation, and withdrawal rates. These simulations provide a clearer picture of how your portfolio might perform under different conditions, helping you understand the risks and trade-offs involved in your financial decisions.

Why Monte Carlo Analysis Matters

Imagine relying on a weather forecast that only predicts tomorrow's temperature. It's helpful, but wouldn't you feel more confident knowing the probability of rain, wind, or a sudden cold snap over the next month? Monte Carlo analysis is like a long-term weather forecast for your finances. It gives you a probability-based understanding of whether your portfolio can support your desired lifestyle, even in challenging economic conditions. Armed with this insight, you can make adjustments—such as fine-tuning spending, adjusting asset allocation, or exploring alternate income streams—to ensure your financial security.

By combining the simplicity of the 4 percent rule with the rigor of tools like Monte Carlo analysis, you can move from broad assumptions to a plan tailored to your specific needs and goals. Confidence in your financial future isn't just about having enough—it's about knowing your plan is built to withstand life's uncertainties.

SWIM Lesson 2

SWIM Lesson:
Prepare for the Descent

Achieving wealth is just one part of the journey. Planning for how to maintain and grow it after reaching your goal is equally important.

ACTION STEP: Write down three potential challenges you foresee in maintaining your wealth. For the first challenge, take one small step today to address it—like scheduling a call with your advisor or researching a solution.

> EXAMPLE:
> - If your challenge is "rising health-care costs," the step could be "call my insurance provider to review my policy."

QUESTION: What are your plans for managing your wealth now that you've reached your financial goals? Do you have a strategy for both growth and protection?

_____

_____

_____

_____

_____

_____

_____

⊕ SWIM Lesson:
Crafting a Second Act

Financial freedom offers the opportunity to design a second act filled with purpose and passion.

ACTION STEP: List two activities or goals that excite you for your next chapter of life. Write down one immediate step to start pursuing one of them.

   EXAMPLE:
   - If you're passionate about travel, research destinations and create a timeline. If you've dreamed of a new business, schedule time to explore feasibility.

QUESTION: How will you use your two-comma wealth to pursue what truly brings you joy and fulfillment in this new phase of life?

_____

_____

_____

_____

_____

_____

_____

_____

_____

_____

_____

⊕ SWIM Lesson:
Overcoming Scarcity Mindset

It can be difficult to move past the fear of spending, even after reaching financial security.

ACTION STEP: Write down one area where you hesitate to spend, despite being able to afford it. Today, choose one small purchase or experience in this area and allow yourself to enjoy it without guilt.

> EXAMPLE:
> - If it's a home improvement, book a consultation with a contractor. If it's travel, set a date to plan the trip.

QUESTION: Are there areas where you hesitate to spend despite being financially able? What steps can you take to give yourself "permission" to enjoy the wealth you've built?

_____

_____

_____

_____

_____

_____

_____

_____

_____

_____

_____

◉ SWIM Lesson: Directional Goals

Think of goals not as destinations but as guideposts along your journey, helping you adjust as circumstances evolve.

ACTION STEP: Identify one long-term goal. Write down the smaller milestones you need to achieve along the way.

EXAMPLE:
- For a goal like retiring to another state, research the location, assess cost of living, and create a timeline for transitioning.

QUESTION: How can you ensure your financial goals remain flexible and adaptable to changes in your life?

_____

_____

_____

_____

_____

_____

_____

_____

_____

_____

_____

_____

⊕ SWIM Lesson:
Protect Your Journey

Wealth is built over a lifetime but can be lost in an instant without proper protections in place.

ACTION STEP: Locate your most recent insurance policy or estate plan. Set a reminder today to review it or email your advisor for an initial assessment.

EXAMPLE:
- If your estate plan is outdated, schedule a meeting with your attorney or advisor to make updates.

QUESTION: What additional steps can you take to safeguard the wealth you've built?

_____

_____

_____

_____

_____

_____

_____

_____

_____

_____

_____

_____

CHAPTER THREE
Assess for Success

The best things in life aren't things.

—ART BUCHWALD

In 2010, economists Daniel Kahneman and Angus Deaton published research showing that for the average American, each additional $1,000 in annual income correlates with greater happiness—up to around $95,000 per year in today's dollars.[9]

After that $95,000 threshold, the study showed that more money doesn't necessarily buy more joy. Sure, you might upgrade from Dunkin' to Starbucks or drive a Lexus instead of a Toyota. But the incremental boost to your quality of life levels off. At a certain point, it's just about buying bigger or nicer stuff, not fundamentally improving your happiness.

The takeaway? My goal is to help you allocate your resources in ways that truly move the needle on what makes you happy. The key to that is discovering what's most important to you (as we discussed in chapter 2) and then taking a clear-eyed look at what's realistically achievable for your situation.

How Realistic Is Your Destination?

Many financial planning books discuss the "latte factor" popularized by author David Bach—the idea that if you saved the money spent on daily coffee purchases, it could eventually turn into a substantial investment.[10] However, I've found that the latte itself is rarely the culprit behind financial troubles. If you already have two-comma wealth and a morning coffee from the Starbucks drive-through brings you joy, then by all means, enjoy it! The same goes for going out to eat with friends—most people, regardless of income level, can find ways to socialize over a meal.

The true financial pitfalls often stem from big-ticket purchases. Even those with two-comma wealth aren't immune. There's an interesting phenomenon on social media where people receive praise from others for posting about their brand-new truck (a depreciating asset), but face scrutiny for sharing photos of a European cruise or some other "exotic" adventure. The societal mindset seems to be that certain expenditures are acceptable while others are not.

When my parents bought a vacation home in the Poconos, my dad encouraged me to buy a property nearby. Against my better judgment, I did—and now we have a second home that we visit maybe once a year. Just this spring, we arrived to find the hot water wasn't working, which, as you can imagine, was not the ideal family vacation. Instead of owning a vacation home, I find myself feeling like this vacation home owns me. Instead of being a place of relaxation, it's a place I feel obligated to visit because of the "investment" made, and the costs continue to pile up.

The true financial pitfalls often stem from big-ticket purchases.

Even at two-comma wealth, this is a common occurrence. People assume the things that got them here will get them there. They were always taught "buy—don't rent" or "own—don't lease." However, there's merit in realizing that things—and the inevitable upkeep that comes with them—can cost us one of our most highly valued possessions: our time.

The reality is that it's the large fixed costs—housing, RVs, boats, cars, land—that can truly weigh you down. A vacation home may sound appealing, but the ongoing maintenance and upkeep can quickly diminish the joy. A fancy convertible may seem like a dream, but if you live in a high-snow state, it could end up sitting unused for most of the year.

Similarly, boat ownership can come with significant hassles around storage, transportation, and maintenance. There's a common saying, however, that the two best days are when you buy a boat and when you sell it. At one time, I did want to own a boat. Whenever we went out on our friend's boat, my family and I had a wonderful time. It was a great way to make memories and have quality family time. But instead of jumping off the deep end into boat ownership myself, I decided to join a boat club where I could pay a set monthly fee and use a boat anytime I wanted. No maintenance, no transporting, and no cleaning. Really, all I have to do is pay for the gas I use that day. I can try out all sorts of boats with no commitment and use any club around the world without having to buy a truck to pull it around in. If I don't want to use a boat anymore, I can just cancel the service. I don't feel beholden to the boat. (Oh, well, we bought a boat, so now we *have to* go to the lake for vacation!) I don't have to go through the hassle of trying to sell a boat. It is convenient, and when we are traveling as a family, all I need to do is look up the marinas in the area where the club exists, and the boat is there waiting for me without me needing to tow it across the country and even in other countries.

The reality is that it's the large fixed costs—housing, RVs, boats, cars, land—that can truly weigh you down.

Now, if, after my experience with the boat club, I decided that I really wanted a boat of my own because we use it all the time, I would have a baseline understanding of what boat ownership really means, with the pros and all of the cons that come along with it.

This type of intermediate step can be very valuable when considering major purchases. Rather than making an in-the-moment decision, it's often wise to explore alternatives that provide the desired experience without the full responsibilities and costs of ownership. This can help ensure I make a well-informed decision that aligns with my long-term goals and lifestyle.

> *Rather than making an in-the-moment decision, it's often wise to explore alternatives that provide the desired experience without the full responsibilities and costs of ownership.*

All that being said, if it turns out after a handful of rented RV trips, a year in a boat club, or a repeated Airbnb visit to the same spot several times in a year that you have found yourself dreaming about and still wanting one of your very own, go for it! Same goes for anything else your two-comma wealth budget affords you because these are now experiences that bring you joy and that you have shown to be a long-term important part of who you are and what you value. The key here is that moments matter, not things, and often, we have spent so much time in the accumulation phase of growing assets, including "stuff," that we think it's the "stuff" that made us happy, and that is rarely, if ever, the case.

Assessing Your Spending Habits

Before committing to a major purchase, I encourage you to assess your needs and usage honestly. The goal should be to strike a balance—not underspending from a scarcity mindset or overspending in a way that compromises your long-term financial health and happiness.

Today's digital age makes it easier than ever to spend without thinking. Amazon's "Buy Now" button, contactless payments, and subscription services are designed to remove any hesitation before purchase. While we don't need to obsess over every penny, a well-maintained budget is essential, even at two-comma wealth. Think of a budget as a tool for intentional living.

Consider using a budget to prevent overspending on things that don't matter while encouraging thoughtful spending on what does. By reviewing your spending habits regularly and discussing them with your financial advisor, you can stay on track and ensure your resources are being used in ways that truly bring you joy.

Think of a budget as a tool for intentional living.

The Impact of Sequence of Returns

The impact of sequence of returns risk is an essential consideration in investment income distribution planning, especially for retirees. This concept demonstrates how the timing of market returns—not just the overall returns—can significantly affect the sustainability of a portfolio during retirement. Consider two retirees, Alice and Bob, who each start with a $1 million portfolio and plan to withdraw $40,000 in their first year, increasing by 3 percent annually to account for inflation. Although the market returns they experience are identical over time, the order in which those returns occur creates vastly different outcomes. If there were no withdrawals, the ending portfolio values would be the same, regardless of the sequence. However, once distributions are introduced, the sequence of returns can profoundly impact long-term results, as we'll see in their examples.

Alice: Positive Returns Early (Fixed Withdrawal)

Alice enjoys strong returns early in her retirement, which helps her portfolio grow despite her annual withdrawals:

YEAR	RETURN	BALANCE START	WITHDRAWAL (3% INFLATION ADJUSTED)	PORTFOLIO VALUE END
1	+20%	$1,000,000	$40,000	$1,160,000
2	+15%	$1,160,000	$41,200	$1,292,800
3	+12%	$1,292,800	$42,436	$1,405,500
4	+8%	$1,405,500	$43,709	$1,474,231
5	-10%	$1,474,231	$45,020	$1,281,787
6	-15%	$1,281,787	$46,371	$1,043,148
7	+10%	$1,043,148	$47,761	$1,099,701
8	+12%	$1,099,701	$49,195	$1,182,470
9	-5%	$1,182,470	$50,671	$1,072,676
10	+6%	$1,072,676	$52,191	$1,084,846

Total Withdrawn: $458,554
Portfolio Value after Ten Years: $1,084,846

Alice's early gains help her portfolio withstand later downturns and continue growing.

Bob: Negative Returns Early (Fixed Withdrawal)

Bob's retirement starts with back-to-back market declines, which negatively impact his portfolio, even though the overall returns are the same as Alice's:

YEAR	RETURN	BALANCE START	WITHDRAWAL (3% INFLATION ADJUSTED)	PORTFOLIO VALUE END
1	-15%	$1,000,000	$40,000	$810,000
2	-10%	$810,000	$41,200	$687,800
3	+12%	$687,800	$42,436	$727,900
4	+8%	$727,900	$43,709	$742,423
5	+20%	$742,423	$45,020	$845,887
6	+15%	$845,887	$46,371	$926,399
7	+10%	$926,399	$47,761	$971,277
8	+12%	$971,277	$49,195	$1,038,635
9	-5%	$1,038,635	$50,671	$936,033
10	+6%	$936,033	$52,191	$940,004

Total Withdrawn: $458,554

Portfolio Value after Ten Years: $940,004

Bob's early losses, combined with steady withdrawals, leave him with $144,842 less than Alice at the end of ten years despite experiencing the same overall returns.

Bob: Negative Returns Early (Dynamic Withdrawal)

To mitigate the effects of early losses, Bob adopts a dynamic withdrawal strategy, reducing his withdrawals by 25 percent in down-market years and returning to inflation-adjusted withdrawals in positive return years.

YEAR	RETURN	BALANCE START	WITHDRAWAL (ADJUSTED)	PORTFOLIO VALUE END
1	-15%	$1,000,000	$30,000 (reduced by 25%)	$820,000
2	-10%	$820,000	$30,900 (reduced by 25%)	$707,100
3	+12%	$707,100	$42,436 (inflation adjusted)	$749,516
4	+8%	$749,516	$43,709 (inflation adjusted)	$765,768
5	+20%	$765,768	$45,020 (inflation adjusted)	$873,902
6	+15%	$873,902	$46,371 (inflation adjusted)	$958,616
7	+10%	$958,616	$47,761 (inflation adjusted)	$1,006,715
8	+12%	$1,006,715	$49,195 (inflation adjusted)	$1,078,326
9	-5%	$1,078,326	$38,003 (reduced by 25%)	$986,407
10	+6%	$986,407	$52,191 (inflation adjusted)	$993,400

Total Withdrawn: $425,586
Portfolio Value after Ten Years: $993,400

By reducing his withdrawals during poor market years, Bob preserves more of his capital. Although his total withdrawals are lower, his portfolio value is significantly better than with the fixed withdrawal strategy.

Bob: Negative Returns Early (Bucket Strategy)

Another strategy Bob could use is the bucket strategy, which divides his assets into three distinct categories based on time horizon:

- BUCKET 1: *Cash Reserve*—$80,000 for two years of withdrawals, allowing him to avoid selling investments during market downturns.
- BUCKET 2: *Bonds*—$300,000 invested in bonds generating 4 percent annually to cover medium-term expenses.
- BUCKET 3: *Stocks*—The remaining $620,000 is invested in stocks for long-term growth.

With the bucket strategy, Bob's portfolio looks like this:

YEAR	STOCK RETURN	WITHDRAWAL (ADJUSTED)	PORTFOLIO VALUE END (BONDS/STOCKS ADJUSTED)
1	-15%	$40,000	$879,000
2	-10%	$41,200	$797,580
3	+12%	$42,436	$823,342
4	+8%	$43,709	$832,115
5	+20%	$45,020	$910,420
6	+15%	$46,371	$974,389
7	+10%	$47,761	$1,011,244
8	+12%	$49,195	$1,070,251
9	-5%	$50,671	$972,625
10	+6%	$52,191	$975,832

Total Withdrawn: $458,554
Portfolio Value after Ten Years: $975,832

The bucket strategy protects Bob from having to sell stocks in down markets, allowing time for his investments to recover. His portfolio remains relatively strong, and his withdrawals remain consistent.

Summary Comparison of Strategies after Ten Years

PERSON	STRATEGY	TOTAL WITHDRAWN	PORTFOLIO VALUE AFTER 10 YEARS
ALICE	FIXED WITHDRAWAL	$458,554	$1,084,846
BOB	FIXED WITHDRAWAL	$458,554	$940,004
BOB	DYNAMIC WITHDRAWAL	$425,586	$993,400
BOB	BUCKET STRATEGY	$458,554	$975,832

Bob's dynamic withdrawal strategy results in a higher ending portfolio balance than the fixed withdrawal and bucket strategies. However, the bucket strategy provides more consistent withdrawals while protecting the portfolio during down markets. Both strategies demonstrate how adjusting withdrawals or employing a structured approach can mitigate the negative effects of poor market returns early in retirement.

Let's explore the numbers together because this is where the real power of these strategies becomes clear.

Alice's fixed withdrawal strategy shows what happens when you start retirement with some good luck—strong market returns early on. Her portfolio grows nicely in the first few years, allowing it to recover from the later downturns. Even with consistent withdrawals adjusted for inflation, Alice ends up with over $1 million after ten years. It's a straightforward approach: she doesn't change her strategy based on the market. This can work well in a best-case scenario, but it's also risky if the market takes a downturn right after you retire. For Alice, it worked out, but for Bob, it's a different story.

Bob's fixed withdrawal strategy reveals the impact of bad luck early in retirement. He experiences market losses in the first few years, and because his withdrawals continue steadily, he finds himself down nearly $150,000 compared to Alice after ten years. The fixed withdrawal strategy is simple, but it can be a bit rigid. The biggest drawback here is that Bob's portfolio struggles to recover from the early losses because he's forced to keep withdrawing the same inflation-adjusted amount, even when the market is down. If you want consistency in your withdrawals, this approach works, but it doesn't protect your portfolio if you face poor market returns early on.

To combat that risk, Bob tries a dynamic withdrawal strategy, where he cuts back on his initial planned withdrawal by 25 percent (likely holding off on many of those wants and wishes) during bad years and takes the full amount in better years. By doing so, he's able to preserve more of his portfolio. After ten years, he's withdrawn less money overall, but his balance is higher—just under $1 million. The tradeoff here is that Bob sacrifices some flexibility in his spending. He has to pull back when the market is struggling, which may be tough if he needs the funds for living expenses. But the advantage is clear: this strategy helps protect the portfolio and reduces the chances of running out of money too soon. If you're comfortable adjusting your withdrawals based on market conditions, this strategy might be a good fit.

Lastly, we have Bob's bucket strategy, which breaks his portfolio into short-term cash, medium-term bonds, and long-term stocks. This approach is a great way to keep the money he needs in the near future safe while giving his long-term investments time to grow. Over the ten years, he withdraws the same amount as in the fixed strategy, but because he pulls from safer investments in the down years, his stock investments have time to recover. At the end of ten years, Bob's portfolio balance is $975,832—lower than with the dynamic strategy but still quite healthy. This method requires a bit more planning upfront, but it provides peace of mind. You don't have to worry about selling stocks at the wrong time because you've already set aside the funds you'll need in the next few years. If you prefer a structured approach and don't want to adjust your spending year to year, the bucket strategy can offer stability. We will discuss more about asset allocation and how I break down the buckets mentioned in the bucket strategy into different lanes of an investment highway in the next chapter.

In the end, there's no single solution that works perfectly for everyone in every scenario. Each strategy has its strengths and trade-offs, and the right choice depends on how comfortable you are with market fluctuations and how flexible you can be with your spending. That's why it's essential to work with a financial advisor who can help craft a plan that suits your lifestyle and goals. This chapter is meant to show the different ways you can enhance your financial outcomes and manage risk based on market performance while also creating a budget that gives you the freedom to spend and the confidence to enjoy each moment. The key is understanding your options and choosing the approach that best suits your needs.

Flexibility and Strategic Planning

It's important to note that while these strategies—fixed withdrawals, dynamic withdrawals, and the bucket approach—can help manage the risk of unfavorable market returns, there are other critical factors to consider in retirement planning. Your personal risk tolerance, lifestyle goals, health, and other financial commitments all play a significant role in shaping the optimal strategy for your unique situation.

There is no universal approach to retirement withdrawals. While this chapter illustrates how different strategies can improve outcomes and mitigate risks, the reality is that each person's circumstances are different. The best approach for you might combine elements from various strategies, or it may involve a completely different method, depending on factors like market conditions, tax considerations, or unexpected life changes.

Another important component of retirement planning for two-comma wealth is *tax-efficient withdrawal sequencing*. By strategically choosing which accounts to draw from first, you can optimize tax outcomes. We will discuss the taxation of account types in chapter 5 but generally, the order of withdrawals might be:

- TAXABLE ACCOUNTS first, drawing down assets that have already been taxed.
- TAX-DEFERRED ACCOUNTS like traditional IRAs and 401(k)s, second, strategically taking withdrawals up to a certain tax bracket or to meet required minimum distributions (RMDs).
- ROTH ACCOUNTS last, as these funds grow tax-free and do not require RMDs.

As portfolios grow in size, so do the complexities of efficient withdrawals. Balancing tax efficiency, market performance, and income needs often requires fine-tuning that changes year to year. An experienced financial advisor can help you navigate these complexities, using tools like detailed cash flow analysis and tax projections to refine your strategy.

Working with a financial advisor can help you formulate a personalized income strategy that aligns with your individual goals and risk tolerance. An advisor can guide you through the complexities of sequencing returns and withdrawal strategies and how to adjust them over time as market conditions and your life circumstances evolve.

SWIM Lesson 3

SWIM Lesson:
Focus on What Truly Brings Joy

Money beyond a certain point doesn't buy more happiness. Use your wealth to prioritize meaningful experiences over material possessions.

ACTION STEP: Write down one material purchase you regret and one experience that brought you lasting joy. Reflect on how this influences your future spending.

> EXAMPLE:
> - You may regret buying an expensive watch that now sits in a drawer but cherish memories of a family trip to Italy. Focus future spending on experiences that build meaningful connections.

QUESTION: What purchases or experiences genuinely improve your quality of life? Are there any areas where you could reduce spending on things that don't bring lasting joy?

_____

_____

_____

_____

_____

_____

_____

⊚ SWIM Lesson:
Assess Spending for Needs, Wants, and Wishes

Use financial planning software or modeling with your financial advisor to assess how your current spending impacts your ability to achieve your needs, wants, and wishes.

ACTION STEP: Work with your financial advisor to model your spending and portfolio performance. Use these insights to identify adjustments—like reallocating spending or refining goals—that can strengthen your financial plan.

> EXAMPLE:
> - A financial model might show that reallocating $10,000 annually from discretionary expenses—such as a high-end car lease—into a dedicated travel fund could enable a luxury vacation each year, all while staying aligned with long-term financial goals.

QUESTION: How does your current spending align with your financial priorities? Could modeling reveal ways to better achieve your needs, wants, and wishes?

_____

_____

_____

_____

_____

_____

_____

_____

⊙ SWIM Lesson:
Assess Big-Ticket Purchases and Try Before You Buy

Big-ticket purchases can come with hidden costs that outweigh their benefits. Starting with smaller or trial versions helps confirm alignment with your goals before committing.

ACTION STEP: Identify one significant purchase you're considering. Create a pros-and-cons list and research a rental, trial, or smaller option to test its fit before fully committing.

Example:
- Thinking of buying an RV? Consider renting one for a road trip to understand the maintenance, driving, and storage aspects before committing to ownership.

QUESTION: How can you test the value of a big purchase and evaluate whether it aligns with your long-term happiness and goals?

_____

_____

_____

_____

_____

_____

_____

_____

_____

⊕ SWIM Lesson:
Manage Sequence of Returns Risk

The timing of market returns during the withdrawal phase can dramatically affect your portfolio's longevity. Strategies like maintaining short-term income investments, rebalancing your portfolio, and diversifying investments can help safeguard against early market downturns.

ACTION STEP: Work with your financial advisor to model your portfolio under different market scenarios. Identify how allocating funds to money markets, treasury bills, CDs, or short-term bond funds could reduce sequence risk.

EXAMPLE:
- If a model shows a 15 percent market drop early in retirement, drawing income from short-term investments like treasury bills or CDs instead of selling stocks can help protect long-term portfolio growth.

QUESTION: How could early market downturns impact your portfolio? Are you taking steps, like rebalancing or using short-term income investments, to protect against sequence of returns risk?

_____

_____

_____

_____

_____

_____

_____

⊕ SWIM Lesson:
Optimize Withdrawal Strategies

Choosing the right withdrawal strategy, such as dynamic withdrawals or a bucket approach, can ensure a steady income while protecting your portfolio from downturns. Tailoring your strategy to your lifestyle and goals is key.

ACTION STEP: Evaluate your withdrawal plan with your financial advisor. Discuss whether a flexible strategy, like adjusting withdrawals based on market conditions or using the bucket approach, could improve your financial outcomes.

> EXAMPLE:
> - If you experience a market downturn early in retirement, using a bucket strategy to draw from bonds instead of stocks could give your portfolio time to recover.

QUESTION: Are you using a withdrawal strategy that balances steady income with long-term portfolio growth? What adjustments could improve your plan's flexibility and resilience?

_____

_____

_____

_____

_____

_____

_____

CHAPTER FOUR

Your Money in Motion

Complexity is your enemy. Any fool can make something
complicated. It is hard to keep things simple.

—RICHARD BRANSON

Y ou've reached the next chapter, both literally and figuratively. With two-comma wealth at your disposal, the world is your oyster. Hopefully, through the first few chapters of this book, you've identified your needs, wants, and wishes and have settled on a withdrawal strategy that matches your risk tolerance and income needs. But now what? It's time to shift gears and put your hard-earned dollars to work, navigating the twists and turns of your financial journey, like setting off on a long, scenic road trip.

You've spent years building your wealth, and now, as you enter your distribution years, the real question becomes: How will you steer your investments down the road ahead? You've got the vehicle, the fuel, and a destination in mind—but the highway of life can throw in a few unexpected detours. Are you ready to handle them?

In the previous chapter, we introduced Alice and Bob. Both began their retirement with $1 million, but their experiences couldn't have been more different. Alice hit the financial jackpot early with strong

How will you

steer your investments

down the

road ahead?

returns that allowed her portfolio to thrive, while Bob encountered a rougher ride, facing early market downturns that slowed his progress. Their stories show just how critical it is not only to have a plan but also to be prepared for the unexpected curves that come your way.

The good news? There are strategies to help smooth out the ride. By diversifying your portfolio and following a plan—like the bucket strategy—you can travel down both smooth highways and bumpy back roads with confidence, knowing you've got the right tools to handle whatever the market throws your way. Buckle up. Because this chapter is all about steering your wealth in the right direction.

The Lanes of Personal Finance

If we were sitting in my office, I'd draw five distinct traffic lanes on the whiteboard to illustrate the diversification of your investment portfolio. Think of your financial journey as traveling on a multi-lane highway, with each lane representing a different investment category to diversify your wealth. Each lane, like a vehicle, serves a specific purpose, moving you toward your destination at varying speeds.

With the bucket strategy in mind, each lane can also represent a different time horizon for your money—some for short-term needs, others for long-term growth.

The Emergency Lane (a.k.a. Cash)

Let's start on the far right, with the emergency lane. The emergency lane is only used when there's an issue that requires immediate attention—like a flat tire or engine trouble. You pull over, assess the situation, and act. In the emergency lane, you're not moving forward; you're stopped to handle a critical need.

In personal finance, this lane represents your cash reserves—your financial cushion for unexpected expenses. In chapter 3, we talked about Bob setting aside as much as one to two years of living expenses in cash. This "emergency lane" of cash or cash equivalents like money markets, money market mutual funds, or high-yield savings and insured bank deposit accounts is essential for keeping you safe when life throws unexpected challenges your way.

Holding too much cash, though, can slow your financial progress, just like spending too much time parked in the emergency lane. Inflation acts like a semitruck barreling down the highway, eroding the value of your cash over time. So, while it's crucial to have enough set aside for emergencies, you don't want to stay in this lane longer than necessary. Your goal is to use it when needed and then get back on the road.

The Bus Lane (a.k.a. Fixed Income)

Next, we have the bus lane, where vehicles move at a slower, steadier pace. This lane is for those who prioritize stability over speed. The bus lane is where your fixed-income investments, such as CDs, bonds, fixed annuities, and certain private debt investments, reside.

This lane aligns with the second bucket in the bucket strategy: income investments. These investments provide steady, predictable returns, acting as a stabilizer during periods of market volatility. For example, Bob relied on his bond investments during the early years of his retirement when the stock market experienced a downturn. By staying in the bus lane, he avoided selling stocks at the worst possible time, allowing his long-term investments to recover.

Fixed-income investments may not be thrilling, but they play a critical role in maintaining

This lane is for those who prioritize stability over speed.

balance and providing peace of mind. They ensure you're making steady progress on your journey, even if inflation occasionally creeps up behind you. However, not all fixed-income investments are created equal.

High-yield bonds, often referred to as "junk bonds," can carry significant risks. These bonds offer higher interest rates but are issued by companies or entities with lower credit ratings. Because of this, they can behave more like equities than traditional fixed-income assets. Similarly, emerging market (EM) debt, which involves bonds issued by governments or corporations in developing countries, can provide attractive yields but comes with heightened risk factors, including the following:

- POLITICAL AND ECONOMIC INSTABILITY: Emerging markets may face unpredictable political events or economic challenges that can affect the issuer's ability to make payments.
- CURRENCY RISK: Many EM bonds are issued in foreign currencies, exposing investors to fluctuations in exchange rates that can amplify losses.
- LIQUIDITY RISK: EM debt markets can be less liquid than developed markets, making it harder to sell these investments during times of financial stress.

While these higher-yield options can diversify a portfolio or boost income, they may not align with the core purpose of the fixed-income lane, which is to provide stability. If you truly want this portion of your portfolio to operate in a "bus lane" fashion, limiting your exposure to high-yield bonds and EM debt is essential.

It's also important to address variable annuities, which are sometimes marketed as fixed-income investments. While some of the sub-accounts within a variable annuity may include income-oriented investments, they don't typically fit the same profile as traditional fixed-income vehicles. Sub-accounts often consist of mutual fund–like investments tied to market performance, meaning their value can fluctuate just like stocks. Additionally, variable annuities may include high fees, surrender charges, and complex features that could detract from their intended purpose. While they can offer benefits such as tax deferral and optional income riders, these products are better categorized as hybrid or market-linked investments rather than as true fixed income.

Another option gaining traction among investors with two-comma wealth is private credit or private equity debt. These investments involve lending to businesses or projects outside traditional public markets. Private credit is often marketed to high-net-worth individuals because of its higher yield potential, exclusivity, and diversification appeal. Many two-comma wealth investors find themselves approached with these opportunities because issuers view them as sophisticated investors who can handle the liquidity constraints and complexity involved. While private credit can offer enticing returns, it also comes with significant risks:

- LIQUIDITY RISK: These investments often have long lock-up periods, meaning you may not access your funds for years. This lack of liquidity can be challenging, particularly if unexpected cash needs arise.
- CREDIT RISK: The borrowers in private credit arrangements may be less established or financially secure than those in traditional fixed-income vehicles, increasing the risk of default.
- COMPLEXITY AND TRANSPARENCY: Private credit agreements are often complex, with limited visibility into the borrower's financial health, the specific terms of the loan, or how the underlying assets are performing.
- REGULATORY OVERSIGHT: These investments lack the regulatory protections of public markets, leaving investors more reliant on their own due diligence or the reputation of the issuer.

While private credit, high-yield bonds, and EM debt might suit certain investors seeking higher yields or portfolio diversification, it's essential to consider whether these opportunities truly align with your financial goals and risk tolerance.

By focusing on high-quality fixed-income investments such as US Treasuries, CDs, and short-term bond funds, your bus lane can provide the stability needed to offset risks in other parts of your portfolio. Always work with a trusted advisor to ensure your fixed-income strategy aligns with your overall plan, keeping the journey smooth and steady.

The Minivan Lane (a.k.a. Growth and Income)

Now we move to the minivan lane. Drivers here are cruising at a comfortable pace—not too fast, but not too slow. This lane represents a balance between safety and functionality.

In the world of investing, this is where your growth-and-income investments—typically large, well-established companies—fit in. Think of companies like Johnson & Johnson or Procter & Gamble. They offer both the potential for capital appreciation and a steady stream of dividends, much like the dependable minivan that comfortably transports your family across the country. Many companies in this lane aim not just to maintain their dividends but to grow them over time, adding to their appeal and helping to keep pace with inflation—like a minivan with adaptive cruise control that adjusts smoothly to the flow of traffic.

It's worth noting, however, that dividends are not guaranteed. Companies can reduce or eliminate them, just as adaptive cruise control slows your car when traffic conditions change. This is unlike bond investments, which are promissory notes with fixed income unless the issuer defaults.

For retirees like Alice and Bob, the minivan lane represents their growth-and-income bucket. These investments provide a balance of growth and stability, giving enough fuel to continue the journey over the long haul while seeking to outrun the inflation "semitruck" that often sideswipes those sitting idly in the cash lane. The minivan lane ensures your portfolio is well-rounded, offering both steady income and moderate growth potential.

Additionally, this lane includes public real estate investment trusts (REITs). Public REITs invest in income-generating real estate, such as commercial properties, apartment buildings, or health-care facilities, and typically pay out a significant portion of their earnings as dividends. Public REITs can offer an attractive source of growth and income, providing diversification to your portfolio and acting as a hedge against inflation.

Private REITs can also be part of the minivan lane, but they come with additional considerations. Like other private investment products, private REITs are less liquid, often requiring long lock-up periods. They may lack the transparency of public REITs, making it harder to gauge performance and assess risks. Furthermore, private REITs can carry higher fees and are not subject to the same level of regulatory oversight, leaving investors more reliant on the issuer's reputation and due diligence.

The risks of private REITs echo those mentioned in the bus lane with private credit and other private investment vehicles:

- **LIQUIDITY RISK:** You may not access your capital for years, depending on the terms of the investment.
- **TRANSPARENCY:** Limited disclosure requirements can make it difficult to evaluate the underlying properties or the overall financial health of the REIT.
- **MANAGEMENT RISK:** The success of a private REIT depends heavily on the expertise and decisions of its management team.
- **MARKET SENSITIVITY:** Although private REITs are less volatile than public REITs, they are not immune to real estate market downturns or shifts in interest rates.

For those with two-comma wealth, private REITs are often marketed as exclusive opportunities, touting their high-potential yields and diversification benefits. However, it's crucial to consider whether these align with your goals and risk tolerance.

By incorporating high-quality public REITs and cautiously considering private REITs when appropriate, you can enhance the balance of income and growth in the minivan lane while keeping your investment journey steady and purposeful.

The Sports Car Lane (a.k.a. Growth)

Move one lane over from the minivan, and you enter the sports car lane—where drivers are moving fast, eager to get ahead. This is for investors willing to take on more risk for the potential of higher rewards.

In this lane, we find growth investments—mid-cap and small-cap stocks that are expected to expand rapidly. These investments prioritize growth over dividends, reinvesting profits to fuel the company's expansion. Think of early-stage companies like Amazon or Tesla in their formative years.

In Alice's portfolio, strong early returns in this lane helped her stay on track and build her wealth. This lane offers the potential for outsized gains, but it also comes with more volatility. Just like driving a sports car at high speeds, you need to be prepared for sudden shifts and sharp turns.

The Sports Bike Lane (a.k.a. Aggressive Growth)

Finally, we have the sports bike lane—where the most daring drivers push the limits, weaving in and out of traffic at high speeds. This lane represents high-risk, high-reward investments like penny stocks, cryptocurrencies, speculative ventures, emerging market equities, and private equity.

Investing in this lane can result in massive gains if everything goes well. However, just like riding a motorcycle at ninety miles per hour, there's little margin for error. A pothole could send you flying, and in the investment world, that pothole could be a significant market downturn, regulatory changes, or unforeseen geopolitical events.

Emerging market equities are an example of investments that can accelerate growth but come with heightened risks. These markets—such as those in Southeast Asia, Latin America, or Africa—offer opportunities to tap into rapidly growing economies. However, they are often more volatile than developed markets and are susceptible to political instability, currency fluctuations, and limited transparency. While emerging market equities can be lucrative, they require a higher risk tolerance and a long-term outlook.

Private equity is another category that often occupies this lane, appealing to those with two-comma wealth due to its exclusive access and potential for outsized returns. Private equity investments involve acquiring stakes in privately held companies, often through specialized funds. While they can offer significant rewards, they also come with considerable risks:

- ILLIQUIDITY: Investments are typically locked up for years, leaving no flexibility to sell if market conditions or personal circumstances change.
- MANAGEMENT AND OPERATIONAL RISK: Success hinges on the management team's ability to turn the company around or grow it effectively.
- HIGH FEES: Private equity funds often have complex fee structures, including management and performance fees, which can eat into returns.
- MARKET SENSITIVITY: Economic downturns can disproportionately affect private equity due to its reliance on leverage and high-growth assumptions.

Alice and Bob might allocate only a small portion of their portfolio to this lane, knowing that while the potential for high returns is enticing, so is the risk of significant losses. For those venturing into this lane, diversification and professional guidance are crucial to mitigate risks.

While the sports bike lane can provide a thrilling ride with the promise of substantial returns, it's essential to recognize the dangers and drive responsibly. A carefully considered allocation to this lane, paired with disciplined risk management, ensures it complements rather than jeopardizes your broader investment strategy.

Which Lane Is Right for You?

The key to a successful financial journey is not sticking to just one lane but strategically moving between them. All the lanes are right for you—when used in the right proportion.

As we saw with Alice and Bob, maintaining balance is key. Bob struggled early on because he didn't have enough reserves in his cash and bond buckets to weather the storm of market losses during his first few distribution years. By using the bucket strategy, you can strategically allocate your assets across the investment lanes—balancing liquidity, income, and growth needs.

If you're nearing or in retirement, it's critical to have a clear understanding of which lanes make the most sense for you. Many with two-comma wealth accumulated their money by taking concentrated risks, perhaps driving mostly in the sports car lane and likely without even realizing it. But now, as you look to preserve your wealth, diversification across the lanes is crucial. Concentration may help you build wealth, but diversification helps you preserve it.

All the lanes are right for you—when used in the right proportion.

Managing Your Journey:
The Bucket Strategy in Action

Concentration may

Think of your journey through retirement like
a well-planned road trip. You'll need to switch *help you build wealth,*
lanes depending on the terrain and conditions.
When the weather's clear, you might speed up, *but diversification*
but when you hit a patch of rough road, you'll
slow down, lean on your reserves, and avoid *helps you preserve it.*
risky maneuvers.

This is exactly how Bob has decided to approach his retirement.
Using the bucket strategy, he divided his portfolios into different
buckets:

- BUCKET 1 *(Emergency Lane)*: Cash reserves for short-term
  needs.
- BUCKET 2 *(Bus Lane)*: Bonds for steady income over the next
  five to ten years.
- BUCKET 3 *(Minivan and Sports Car Lanes)*: Growth-and-income
  investments, plus high-growth stocks for long-term growth.

Whenever the market hit a rough patch, he relied on his emergency
and bond buckets to avoid selling stocks at a loss. When conditions
improve, he will reallocate gains from the growth lane to refill their
reserves. This systematic approach gives him confidence that he can
stay on the road and continue on to his destination, no matter the
market conditions.

A Balanced Approach for the Long Haul

Your journey through retirement is like a road trip with many twists and turns. Thoughtful diversification is an important tool for navigating this ride, helping to smooth out the bumps that could otherwise slow you down or derail your progress. Market volatility is part of the trip—Warren Buffett said it best: "The stock market is a device for transferring money from the impatient to the patient." While speeding ahead can lead to higher returns over time, the volatility along the way can be unsettling during market downturns, making it hard to stay the course.

By spreading your investments across different lanes—some focused on income, others on growth—you can build a portfolio that adapts to changing conditions and keeps you on track toward your goals. This strategy allows you to patiently ride out market turbulence and take advantage of opportunities to rebalance. The classic "buy low, sell high" mantra can be difficult without diversification, but by investing in different assets that move at different speeds, you can rebalance during those market traffic jams. Think of it like driving: When one lane stops and another starts moving, it's tempting to switch lanes. But we all know what happens next—as soon as you switch, your new lane grinds to a halt, and the old one zooms by. This is a reminder to resist the urge to jump in and out of markets, trying to time them perfectly—a nearly impossible task.

It's hard not to follow the crowd when the investments we're holding aren't performing as expected. But if they're still quality investments

By spreading your investments across different lanes—some focused on income, others on growth—you can build a portfolio that adapts to changing conditions and keeps you on track toward your goals.

that have temporarily dropped in price, that's the time to buy more, not less. Rebalancing allows you to do just that. On the flip side, it can be difficult to sell investments that have outperformed, but it's important to zoom out, see the bigger picture, and stick to the plan you've mapped out. The goal is balance—not being too aggressive or too cautious. By setting guardrails and regularly monitoring each lane's performance, you can optimize your portfolio. For instance, you might set a rule to move 5 percent from cash or fixed income into growth assets if the stock market drops by 10 percent or more. You can also create similar rules for when your cash reserves or income lanes start to fall behind. This helps you stay disciplined and avoid emotional reactions to big market swings, which can feel very different when you're dealing with two-comma wealth. After all, the percentage returns may stay the same, but six-figure portfolio fluctuations can hit differently than they did before.

Whether you're cruising in the steady income lane or enjoying the thrill of the growth lane, each has its purpose. Finding the right balance between risk and stability is the key to managing your two-comma wealth.

As Bob's experience showed us, it's not just about how much you have—it's about how you manage it across these lanes. Strategies like the bucket system and proper diversification can give you the confidence to handle whatever road you choose. Now that you've picked the right lanes for your journey, we'll talk about which roads come with the highest costs and how to map out the most efficient route to wherever you want your two-comma wealth to take you.

SWIM Lesson 4

SWIM Lesson:
Diversify Across Financial "Lanes"

Just as a highway has multiple lanes for different speeds, your portfolio should be diversified across various asset classes based on your financial goals and risk tolerance. Diversification helps balance short-term needs with long-term growth.

ACTION STEP: Review your portfolio and ensure it includes a mix of cash, fixed-income, growth-and-income, and growth investments to meet your immediate and future goals.

> EXAMPLE:
> - Jordan adjusted his portfolio after realizing he was overexposed to growth investments. By adding more fixed-income assets, he reduced his risk and gained peace of mind during volatile markets.

QUESTION: How well is your portfolio diversified across different investment "lanes"? Are there areas where you could improve balance or reduce concentration?

_____

_____

_____

_____

_____

_____

⊕ SWIM Lesson:
Balance Risk and Stability

Growth investments can provide significant returns, but it's crucial to maintain a balance between riskier assets and stable income sources.

ACTION STEP: Evaluate your portfolio's allocation across various asset classes. Discuss with your financial advisor whether your current balance provides the stability you need during volatile markets.

> EXAMPLE:
> - Cathy allocated 40 percent of her portfolio to fixed-income assets like bonds and 30 percent to high-quality dividend-paying stocks to balance her growth and aggressive growth investments, which gave her confidence to stay invested during a market downturn.

QUESTION: Have you allocated enough of your portfolio to more stable assets like bonds or cash reserves to weather potential market downturns? Does your current allocation between growth and income give you confidence to stay the course?

_____

_____

_____

_____

_____

_____

_____

⦾ SWIM Lesson:
Use the Bucket Strategy for Retirement Planning

Dividing your assets into buckets for short-term needs, medium-term income, and long-term growth helps manage market fluctuations and maintain financial stability in retirement.

ACTION STEP: Organize your investments into buckets based on your spending needs and time horizons. Ask your financial advisor to help you assess whether your current buckets align with your retirement timeline.

> EXAMPLE:
> - Taylor used a bucket strategy, allocating two years of living expenses in cash (Bucket 1), five to ten years of income needs in bonds (Bucket 2), and the rest in stocks for long-term growth (Bucket 3), helping him avoid panic selling during a downturn.

QUESTION: How effectively does your bucket strategy align with your financial needs and goals? Are there areas where you could adjust for better flexibility or stability?

_____

_____

_____

_____

_____

_____

_____

◈ SWIM Lesson:
Know when to Switch "Lanes"

Different market conditions call for adjustments in your investment strategy. Shifting between growth-and-income assets can help you stay on track while maintaining balance.

ACTION STEP: Reflect on your reaction to market changes. Set clear guardrails or rules with your financial advisor to help you make disciplined, systematic portfolio adjustments.

EXAMPLE:
- When the stock market dropped by 10 percent, Alice followed her guardrails and moved 5 percent from cash into growth investments, capitalizing on lower prices instead of panicking.

QUESTION: Do you have a plan for adjusting your portfolio in response to changing market conditions or personal circumstances? What guardrails or rules have you put in place to ensure you are buying low and selling high while staying diversified?

_____

_____

_____

_____

_____

_____

_____

_____

_____

⊕ SWIM Lesson:
Preserving Wealth Through Diversification

Concentrating your assets may have helped build your wealth, but diversifying is essential for making it last during retirement.

ACTION STEP: Reflect on whether your current diversification strategy supports your goals for maintaining financial stability.

EXAMPLE:
- Jay transitioned from a portfolio of tech stocks to a diversified mix of asset classes and sectors, ensuring his wealth could weather market volatility and sustain his retirement income.

QUESTION: How does your current diversification strategy help you balance preservation and growth? Are there areas where you might adjust to better meet your financial goals?

_____

_____

_____

_____

_____

_____

_____

_____

_____

_____

CHAPTER FIVE

Navigating Taxes for Two-Comma Wealth

The hardest thing to understand in the world is the income tax.

—ALBERT EINSTEIN

U p to this point, we've mapped out your needs, wants, and wishes—the destinations along your journey to your next financial summit. In chapter 4, we explored the different financial lanes you can travel in—each with its own speed, purpose, and level of risk. Now, we shift focus to the roads themselves—how the types of accounts you use, and the taxes that come with them, shape the route you take. Some roads are smooth. Others are full of tolls. And just like in any growing city, it's easy to get lost without clear guidance.

Even Einstein admitted the tax system was hard to understand. If he thought it was complicated, the rest of us could use help. Think of this section as a look at the tax and estate planning infrastructure beneath your journey. These financial roads are always under

This book is your printed map—review the routes, then let your financial, legal, and tax advisors guide the way forward.

construction—some expanded, others rerouted or closed without notice, and tax law changes continually reshape the landscape. These next few chapters act like a printed map: they help you zoom out, see where you are, and understand your strategic options using tax laws and rules as they exist at the time of writing. Like any printed map, they eventually become outdated. That's why it's important not to rely solely on these examples, but to use them as a framework for thinking strategically. Then, work with a team of financial, legal, and tax advisors who travel these roads often and can help you avoid detours and find the best route forward.

Maximizing Wealth, Minimizing Tolls

A few years ago, I worked with a young client who inherited $3 million from his aunt—mostly in a traditional IRA. His previous financial advisor suggested using the IRS's ten-year rule for withdrawals, which sounded great on paper. Let it grow for ten years at a projected 7 percent rate, and by then, it would double to $6 million. Sounds good, right?

Not quite. By the end of the decade, my client would have potentially faced a whopping $2.1 million tax bill on his $6 million inheritance because the delay would have pushed him to the highest tax bracket for the majority of the inheritance. He didn't need the money right away; he was in his twenties, living on a modest salary of $30,000 a year. After his dad referred him to me, we worked together with his CPA to revise the plan.

Instead of letting the IRA grow untouched, we chose systematic withdrawals and prioritized maximizing contributions to his Roth 401(k) and Roth IRAs over the ten years. This strategy helped him stay within the more favorable 22 percent and 24 percent tax brackets, saving over $600,000 in taxes on RMDs. Additionally, by moving nearly $300,000 into Roth accounts over those ten years, he set the stage for decades of tax-free growth, resulting in substantial tax savings that could compound significantly over his lifetime—and even be passed to future generations completely tax-free, effectively ending the tax cycle on those assets. Not bad for simply navigating the toll roads

A little tax planning

goes a long way.

smarter. A little tax planning goes a long way. By understanding the tax code, you can save yourself significant amounts of money, which you can use to further grow your wealth.

Putting Your Wealth to Work

In the United States, taxes are based on income, not wealth. This might seem like a subtle difference, but it's a key point for anyone with significant assets. While your overall wealth—the value of everything you own—isn't directly taxed each year, the income that your wealth generates is, whether it's from wages, distributions from tax-deferred accounts, dividends, interest, or capital gains. That means how you manage and structure your income can make a big difference when it comes to taxes.

When you have

Take Warren Buffett, for example. He famously pointed out that he pays a lower tax rate than his secretary, even though he has far more wealth. How? Buffett's income largely comes from capital gains and dividends, which are taxed at lower rates (typically 15–20 percent), whereas his secretary's income, earned as wages, is taxed at ordinary income rates, which can go as high as 37 percent. This example highlights how much of a difference it can make to

two-comma wealth,

it's not just about

making money—it's

about keeping as much

of it as you can.

understand how your income is taxed and why smart planning can reduce your tax burden.

When you have two-comma wealth, it's not just about making money—it's about keeping as much of it as you can. Tax efficiency becomes a critical part of your overall financial plan. There are several strategies you can use to help with this, like converting a traditional IRA to a Roth IRA, taking advantage of charitable giving to offset taxes, or using tax-loss harvesting to reduce your taxable income. These are all practical tools that can make a big difference over time.

Has your financial advisor ever asked for your tax return or discussed tax strategies with you?

Here's a question you might want to ask yourself: Has your financial advisor ever asked for your tax return or discussed tax strategies with you? If not, you could be leaving money on the table. Taxes and your financial plan go hand in hand, and reducing your tax burden is one of the most impactful ways to protect and grow your wealth.

In the next section, we'll break down these strategies in more detail. We'll look at how timing capital gains, charitable contributions, and Roth conversions can all help you pay less in taxes and keep more of your hard-earned wealth working for you. Let's dive into these strategies and see how they can help you.

Tax Brackets and Effective Rates

Let's get the lay of the land: tax brackets and effective rates. Your marginal tax bracket is the rate you pay on your last dollar of income, while your effective tax rate is the average percentage of your total income that you pay in taxes.

For example, a married couple filing jointly in 2025 would have a standard deduction of $30,000. If their income is $150,000, their federal taxable income falls to $120,000, placing them in the 22 percent marginal bracket; but thanks to deductions and the progressive system, their effective rate is about 11 percent. Even as income rises, your effective rate remains below your marginal rate.

Now, here's where it gets interesting for those with two-comma wealth: If you can keep your taxable income within certain lower brackets, your long-term capital gains (those held for over a year) may be taxed at zero percent. That's right—zero percent. We'll dive deeper into this strategy later in the chapter, but for now, let's cover the basics.

Your marginal tax bracket is the rate you pay on your last dollar of income, while your effective tax rate is the average percentage of your total income that you pay in taxes.

Asset Allocation Versus Asset Location

In financial planning, there are two big concepts: asset allocation and asset location. Think of asset allocation as choosing the investment lane you're driving in—stocks, bonds, real estate, etc. Each serves a different purpose, whether it's for growth or income generation.

Asset location, on the other hand, is all about which road you choose to drive on. Are you taking the turnpike (tax-deferred accounts), the scenic back road (tax-free accounts), or the toll road (taxable accounts)? Each one has different tax implications, and your goal is to make sure you're taking the most efficient route for your situation.

Let's look at these routes in more detail.

Tax-Deferred Accounts [Traditional IRAs, 401(k)s]: The Turnpike

These accounts are like a turnpike —you won't pay tolls (taxes) until you exit (withdraw funds). But when you do, the toll is steeper the longer you are on the road, and, thus, the larger the investments in this account grow. Withdrawals are taxed as ordinary income, and required minimum distributions (RMDs) currently begin at age seventy-three, whether you need the money or not.

WHAT TO HOLD HERE: Bonds and nonqualified dividend-paying stocks are great for tax-deferred accounts because they generate income that would otherwise be taxed every year and do so at ordinary income rates anyway. By deferring taxes, you can let these investments grow quietly in the background until retirement.

SPECIAL NOTE: Qualified dividends are dividends from US corporations or qualified foreign corporations that meet certain IRS criteria, and they are taxed at the lower long-term capital gains rates (for now, those rates are zero percent, 15 percent, or 20 percent, depending on your income). Nonqualified dividends are dividends that don't meet these criteria, such as those from REITs and certain foreign companies, and they are taxed at ordinary income tax rates, which can be significantly higher.

Where to hold them for tax efficiency:

- QUALIFIED DIVIDENDS: Best held in taxable accounts (or possibly Roth IRAs) because they benefit from the lower tax rates.
- NONQUALIFIED DIVIDENDS: Ideal for tax-advantaged accounts like IRAs or 401(k)s, where the higher tax rates are deferred until withdrawal.

Tax-Free Growth Accounts [Roth IRA and Roth 401(k)]: The Scenic Back Road

A Roth IRA is like discovering a scenic back road with no tolls—you pay your taxes upfront and then enjoy tax-free growth and withdrawals for the rest of the journey (as long as IRS rules are followed). This makes it an ideal spot for high-growth assets like stocks, especially if you expect them to appreciate over time. The account is named after Senator William Roth, who, in a not-so-subtle move, made sure his legacy would live on in your retirement planning. Historically, the tricky part has been getting large sums into these Roth accounts due to contribution limits, but don't worry—there are a few clever detours, like the backdoor Roth and mega backdoor Roth, that can help you boost those contributions and maximize the benefits of this tax-free road. Let's explore how to make the most of these strategies.

WHAT TO HOLD HERE: Growth stocks and other assets with significant potential for appreciation. You'll pay no taxes on the gains, making this a powerful tool for long-term wealth accumulation.

BONUS STRATEGY: Roth conversions. Convert assets from a traditional IRA to a Roth while your income is lower, like early retirement, and enjoy tax-free growth in the future. Just be careful not to convert so much that you bump into a higher tax bracket! Optimize this strategy during market downturns where you can turn the lemons of a down market into lemonade by converting the same number of shares at a lower cost and thus lower tax payment and have them grow back tax-free in the Roth account when the market recovers.

If you're earning more than the income limits, contributing to a Roth IRA might seem out of reach—but there are still creative ways to make it happen. Let's explore three popular strategies: the Roth IRA, the backdoor Roth IRA, and the rather boldly named mega backdoor Roth (yes, that's the actual name!).

First, the Roth IRA: It's a fantastic tool for tax-free growth and withdrawals in retirement. However, in 2025, if your modified adjusted gross income (MAGI) exceeds $165,000 (for single filers) or $246,000 (for married couples filing jointly), you won't be able to make direct contributions. And even if you qualify, the current contribution limit is $7,000 (or $8,000 if you're fifty or older), which may not feel like enough if you're aiming to save aggressively.

WHY IT MATTERS: Given the growing federal deficit, current tax policies may not be sustainable, and tax rates may need to increase to support rising debt and spending. A Roth account allows you to pay taxes upfront, shielding your future withdrawals from potentially higher rates. This can be especially advantageous if your retirement income remains substantial or if tighter tax brackets emerge in response to fiscal challenges.

It all comes down to a simple question: Do you want to pay tax on the seed or the harvest? With a Roth account, you pay tax on the seed you plant today, ensuring your entire harvest is tax-free later. A traditional IRA account, on the other hand, lets you defer taxes on the seed but requires you to pay on the harvest. The right choice depends on whether you expect to pay lower taxes now or if you and your heirs will face higher taxes on a larger balance in the future.

Even as a high-income earner, choosing to pay taxes on the seed now can create a powerful long-term benefit of tax-free growth potential for you and your heirs. You can also think of it as a forced savings mechanism: by paying taxes upfront, you're effectively contributing more to your retirement savings. With a traditional IRA account, unless you take the tax savings and invest them wisely in a brokerage account, you'd likely end up with less at retirement after taxes, even if tax rates remained exactly the same—because you effectively wouldn't have been contributing as much. Let's now discuss strategies to help you maximize this approach, no matter your income level.

For high earners, the backdoor Roth IRA offers a clever work-around. Here's how it works: you contribute to a traditional IRA (which doesn't have income limits) and then convert that contribution to a

Roth IRA. Since you've already paid taxes on the money, the conversion is generally tax-free. This allows you to bypass the income limits and still enjoy the benefits of a Roth account. Be sure to work with your tax professional and timely file tax Form 8606 registering the nondeductible contribution. This step is often missed by tax preparers and is important to complete the backdoor Roth conversion process and ensure it will not become double taxed.

Now for the mega backdoor Roth—as powerful as its bold name suggests. This strategy lets you contribute after-tax dollars to your 401(k) and then convert those funds into a Roth IRA or Roth 401(k). With the potential to contribute up to $70,000 in 2025 (or $77,500 if you're fifty or older), this method allows high earners to funnel a substantial amount into a Roth account, even if they're disqualified from direct contributions due to income limits.

So, whether you're using a Roth IRA, a backdoor Roth, or going all in with the mega backdoor Roth, these strategies give you the flexibility to grow your retirement savings tax-free, no matter how high your tax bracket may be in the future.

Whether you're using a Roth IRA, a backdoor Roth, or going all in with the mega backdoor Roth, these strategies give you the flexibility to grow your retirement savings tax-free, no matter how high your tax bracket may be in the future.

As you consider how to balance growth and tax efficiency in your portfolio, tools like Roth IRAs shine for their long-term tax-free growth potential. However, there's another account type that deserves attention for its unmatched versatility in addressing health-care costs while offering even greater tax advantages—the health savings account (HSA).

Triple Tax-Advantaged Accounts (HSAs):
The Service Road

Health care can be one of the most significant and unpredictable financial challenges, often derailing even the best-laid plans. The health savings account (HSA) serves as a service road for emergencies, offering a clear and efficient way to navigate these costs without compromising your broader financial strategy. Despite its name, at two-comma wealth, the HSA should not be treated as a savings account. Instead, it should be viewed as an investment vehicle uniquely designed to tackle health-care costs with unmatched tax efficiency.

The HSA's triple tax-free advantage is what sets it apart. Contributions reduce taxable income today, funds grow tax-free while invested, and withdrawals for qualified medical expenses are also tax-free. This trifecta is almost unparalleled in the financial world, making the HSA an invaluable tool for long-term planning. Eligibility for an HSA requires enrollment in a high-deductible health plan, defined in 2025 as having a minimum deductible of $1,650 for individuals or $3,300 for families. Contributions are currently capped at $4,300 for individuals and $8,550 for families annually, with an additional $1,000 catch-up contribution for those aged 55 and older. While the contribution limits may appear modest, their true potential lies in compounding growth over time.

Imagine a couple who contributes just $8,300 annually starting at age 40. By investing their HSA in a diversified portfolio earning an average annual return of 7 percent, their account grows to approximately $755,000 by age seventy. That represents $515,000 in additional potentially tax-free assets compared to spending the funds as they go. Treating your HSA as an investment vehicle rather than a spending account unlocks its true potential and aligns it with the strategic goals of two-comma wealth families.

For those with significant wealth, an additional layer of strategy is available. By using after-tax income or investment proceeds to cover health-care costs out of pocket, you allow the HSA to remain fully invested, compounding tax-free. Later in life, you can reimburse yourself for those earlier expenses tax-free, creating a flexible and efficient source of cash flow when health-care expenses are likely to increase. This approach preserves the HSA for its most impactful use while taking full advantage of its tax benefits.

WHAT TO HOLD HERE: HSAs are ideally suited for growth-oriented investments such as index funds, ETFs, or other diversified equity investments. These assets benefit most from the account's tax-free compounding and long-term focus. Conversely, low-return assets like cash or short-term bonds are generally not ideal for HSAs unless you plan to withdraw the funds in the near future. For two-comma wealth families, the objective is to maximize growth and let the HSA fulfill its role as a long-term investment vehicle. Think of this account as the ideal home for investments with high growth potential rather than a reserve for immediate needs.

STAYING ORGANIZED: To capitalize on the HSA's flexibility, staying organized is essential. Medical expenses reimbursed from the account must occur after it is established, making accurate record-keeping critical. A simple yet effective strategy is to create a dedicated email folder or account for storing digital receipts, payment confirmations, and benefit explanations. This habit ensures you can reimburse yourself seamlessly, even decades later, while allowing the account to remain invested for growth.

HSAs are not simply a tool for covering medical bills; they are a cornerstone of tax-efficient planning. By treating your HSA as a service road for emergencies and an investment vehicle, you can prepare for health-care detours without losing sight of your broader financial journey.

Taxable Accounts (Brokerage Accounts): The Toll Road

Think of taxable accounts like toll roads—every time you make a move, you'll face some tax "tolls" on interest, dividends, and capital gains. However, there are smart strategies to reduce or even avoid some of these tolls. You've probably heard of tax-loss harvesting, which helps minimize taxes by selling underperforming investments to offset gains. But there's another, often-overlooked strategy that can be even more powerful: tax-gain harvesting.

Capital Gain and Loss Harvesting

Most investors are familiar with tax-loss harvesting—selling investments that are down to offset gains elsewhere in your portfolio and reduce taxable income. A lesser-known but equally powerful strategy is tax-gain harvesting, which uses the tax code to pay taxes at the zero percent federal rate on long-term capital gains. That's right—by planning carefully, you can sell appreciated investments and pay zero federal tax on the gains, creating a tax-efficient opportunity to reset your cost basis for future flexibility.

Let's break it down with an example. Consider an early retiree couple in 2025, enjoying a low-income year. Their only income is $15,000 from a CD, taxed at ordinary income rates. To maximize their federal tax efficiency, they decide to harvest $100,000 in long-term capital gains from their taxable portfolio.

Here's how it works under the 2025 tax brackets:

- The standard deduction for a married couple filing jointly is $30,000, reducing their $115,000 total income ($15,000 from interest + $100,000 from capital gains) to $85,000 taxable income.
- The zero percent federal long-term capital gains tax rate applies to taxable income up to $96,700 for married couples

filing jointly. This means the full $100,000 in capital gains falls under the zero percent federal tax bracket, resulting in no federal taxes owed on those gains.

By strategically

realizing gains in these

In fact, the couple has an additional $11,700 of space in the zero percent long-term capital gains bracket ($96,700 threshold minus $85,000 taxable income). This means they could harvest another $11,700 in long-term capital gains, again paying zero federal taxes, while further resetting their cost basis.

low-income years, you

can reset the cost basis

on your investments.

By strategically realizing gains in these low-income years, you can reset the cost basis on your investments.

This isn't about avoiding taxes—it's about using the tax code to your advantage. Paying tax at the zero percent rate is one of the most efficient ways to manage your wealth, especially during low-income years. A proactive financial advisor will take the time to understand your income situation and help craft a strategy like this to ensure you maximize these opportunities.

Working closely with both your advisor and your CPA can make this process seamless. It's especially important to revisit this strategy toward the end of the year, when your income projections are more accurate. A little planning goes a long way, but guesswork can lead to unintended consequences, so professional guidance is key to getting it right.

This strategy complements more commonly known approaches like tax-loss harvesting, where up to $3,000 of capital losses can offset ordinary income each year. But tax-gain harvesting allows you to take full advantage of the zero percent federal tax rate, often overlooked in wealth management discussions. By leveraging this lesser-known tool, you not only lock in tax-free gains but also prepare your portfolio for future growth, creating a win-win scenario for long-term financial success.

What to Hold in a Taxable Account

To minimize the tax "tolls," it's smart to hold investments that offer more control over taxable events, such as individual stocks and ETFs. These tend to be more tax-efficient than mutual funds, which can trigger unexpected capital gains through the manager's trades. Also, understanding the difference between qualified dividends (which are taxed at the favorable capital gains rate) and nonqualified dividends (which are taxed as ordinary income) is crucial. Holding tax-efficient investments can significantly reduce the tax drag on your portfolio.

Tax-Free Investment Products

In addition to tax-efficient investments like individual stocks and ETFs, there are tax-free investment products such as municipal bonds, municipal bond funds, and tax-free money market accounts that can provide attractive income for those in higher tax brackets. These investments are particularly beneficial because the interest they generate is exempt from federal income taxes and, in some cases, state and local taxes if you invest in bonds from your home state.

- MUNICIPAL BONDS are debt securities issued by state and local governments to fund public projects. The key benefit is that the interest is tax-free at the federal level and possibly at the state and local levels as well.
- MUNICIPAL BOND FUNDS pool money from many investors to buy a diversified portfolio of municipal bonds. They provide

broader exposure to various bonds, spreading risk across different issuers.

- **TAX-FREE MONEY MARKET ACCOUNTS** invest in short-term municipal bonds, offering stability and liquidity, much like traditional money markets, but with the added advantage of being free from federal income tax.

Now, how do these tax-free products stack up against their taxable counterparts? When you're in a higher tax bracket, the tax-free income can be more valuable than the higher yields offered by taxable investments. Remember: It's not about what you earn, it's about what you keep. To compare the two, you can use the tax-equivalent yield formula:

$$\text{Tax-Equivalent Yield} = \text{Tax-Free Yield}/(1-\text{Tax Rate})$$

For example, let's say a municipal bond is offering a 3 percent tax-free yield, and you're in the 37 percent marginal federal tax bracket. The tax-equivalent yield would be:

$$\text{Tax-Equivalent Yield} = 3\%/(1-0.37) = 4.76\%$$

This means that a taxable bond would need to offer a yield of 4.76 percent to match the tax-free benefit of a 3 percent municipal bond. The higher your tax bracket, the more beneficial tax-free products can become. In low tax brackets, the opposite is true. You have to do the math to see which makes more sense for you. However, it's important to note that these tax-free investments are only beneficial in taxable accounts. Holding them in an IRA or other tax-deferred accounts would defeat the purpose, as the interest would go from tax-free to taxable upon distribution,

Remember: It's not about what you earn, it's about what you keep.

and you'd be getting paid a lower yield with no tax benefit to offset it. You wouldn't want to hold tax-free bonds in a Roth because the tax benefits are redundant—you're already getting tax-free growth within the Roth, so holding tax-free bonds in it wastes that advantage.

For high-income earners (like the one in our formula example), these products can also help reduce exposure to the alternative minimum tax (AMT) and the net investment income tax (NIIT)—both of which can feel like "speeding tickets" for earning too much on the already expensive toll road you're driving on. Similar to how speeding fines are imposed for going too fast, the AMT and NIIT serve as penalties for crossing certain income thresholds. We'll discuss IRMAA (income-related monthly adjustment amount) later, which operates in a similar way for Medicare premiums. And because investing in municipal bonds helps fund local governments, it's almost like adding a PBA sticker to your car—showing you support the cause and perhaps even helping you avoid getting pulled over in the first place! Just be sure to double-check whether the bonds are private activity bonds, as those may still trigger the AMT and could also be subject to the NIIT, even though they remain federally tax-exempt. Most municipal bonds, however, are free from both AMT and NIIT, offering additional tax efficiency and helping you avoid these "speed traps."

For high-income earners looking for ways to minimize their tax liability, these products can offer attractive, steady income while keeping Uncle Sam at bay.

As we conclude this overview of tax strategies for two-comma wealth, it's clear that navigating this complex landscape requires both knowledge and careful planning. We've explored various "roads" in our financial journey—from the tax-deferred turnpikes of traditional IRAs and 401(k)s to the scenic and toll-free back roads of Roth accounts and the sometimes costly but necessary toll roads of taxable brokerage accounts. But there's an often-overlooked cost that has nothing to do with Uncle Sam at all: investment costs.

Shortcut or Detour?
The True Cost of Investment Choices

When navigating the road to financial success, managing costs is one of the few elements within your control. While active management often promises a shortcut to better returns, there's no guarantee it will outperform passive strategies over the long term. Similarly, directly owning individual securities can provide better tax control and eliminate manager fees, offering another compelling option for reducing costs.

Some asset classes may warrant the expertise of active managers, particularly in less efficient markets. In others, passive strategies like ETFs or index funds can offer lower-cost, effective exposure. Meanwhile, directly owning individual stocks and bonds can give you greater control over taxes and reduce ongoing fees. When comparing options, it's also crucial to evaluate institutional share classes, which often provide the same fund at a lower expense ratio, delivering cost savings without changing the investment strategy.

This is where the value of a good financial advisor comes into play. As noted in chapter 1 and supported by Vanguard's Advisor Alpha® study, an advisor can help uncover efficiently priced investment options, ensuring you're not paying more than necessary to achieve your goals. By balancing active management, passive strategies, and direct ownership, they can tailor your portfolio to align with your objectives while keeping costs in check. Over time, these savings can compound significantly, enhancing your overall financial outcomes.

Wrapping It All Up: The Road Ahead

Managing taxes and costs is a journey, not a destination. Every decision you make—from asset location to selecting the right investment strategy—compounds over time, shaping the trajectory of your wealth. By prioritizing tax efficiency, controlling costs, and leveraging the expertise of a trusted financial advisor, you can preserve more of what you've earned while aligning your portfolio with your financial goals.

As Einstein wisely noted, income tax is one of the hardest things to understand—and it only becomes more intricate as your wealth grows. The strategies we've discussed so far are just the beginning. In the next chapter, we'll explore advanced techniques tailored for two-comma wealth, equipping you with the tools to navigate complex financial decisions and further optimize your tax situation.

So, buckle up. The road ahead may be complex, but with the right knowledge, strategies, and guidance, you'll be well-prepared to navigate it successfully and make the most of your journey.

SWIM Lesson 5

SWIM Lesson:
Understand Tax Brackets and Effective Rates

Tax brackets determine the rate you pay on your last dollar of income, while your effective tax rate is the average percentage of your total income paid in taxes. Knowing these rates is essential for tax planning and financial decisions.

ACTION STEP: Calculate your current marginal and effective tax rates. Reflect on how these rates might influence your investment and withdrawal strategies.

> EXAMPLE:
> - Sam worked with his advisor to stay within the 24 percent tax bracket during his high-income years, reducing his effective tax rate by maximizing deductions and retirement contributions.

QUESTION: How well do you understand your current marginal tax bracket and effective tax rate? How might understanding these affect your financial decisions?

_____

_____

_____

_____

_____

_____

⊕ SWIM Lesson:
Optimize Asset Location for Tax Efficiency

Placing your assets in tax-deferred, tax-free, or taxable accounts strategically can significantly reduce your overall tax liability.

ACTION STEP: Review your asset location strategy to ensure your investments are placed in the most tax-efficient accounts for their type.

EXAMPLE:
- Jamie moved dividend-paying stocks into her Roth IRA, ensuring tax-free growth and withdrawals in retirement, while placing bonds in her traditional IRA to defer taxes on interest income.

QUESTION: Are your investments allocated to the most tax-efficient accounts? What adjustments might improve your tax efficiency?

_____

_____

_____

_____

_____

_____

_____

_____

_____

_____

⊕ SWIM Lesson:
Leverage Tax-Free Growth Opportunities

Roth IRAs and Roth 401(k)s offer tax-free growth and withdrawals, making them powerful tools for long-term wealth accumulation.

ACTION STEP: Evaluate your current use of Roth accounts. Explore strategies like backdoor Roth conversions or mega backdoor Roth contributions to maximize your tax-free savings.

EXAMPLE:
- Ben used a Roth conversion during a market downturn, paying lower taxes on the converted amount while positioning the funds for tax-free growth in his Roth IRA.

QUESTION: Are you maximizing tax-free growth opportunities like Roth accounts? What additional steps could you take to increase your tax-free savings?

_____
_____
_____
_____
_____
_____
_____
_____
_____
_____
_____

⊙ SWIM Lesson:
Implement Tax-Gain Harvesting Strategies

Taking advantage of low-income years to realize capital gains at a zero percent tax rate can reset your cost basis and save on future taxes.

ACTION STEP: Identify a low-income year where tax-gain harvesting might apply. Work with your financial advisor and tax professional to determine if realizing gains could benefit your long-term tax situation.

> EXAMPLE:
> - Amy sold appreciated stock during a sabbatical year, realizing capital gains tax-free, and reinvested the proceeds at a higher cost basis for future tax savings.

QUESTION: How might tax-gain harvesting help you reduce your tax burden in future years? Are there opportunities to take advantage of this strategy now?

_____

_____

_____

_____

_____

_____

_____

_____

_____

_____

SWIM Lesson: Explore Tax-Free Investment Products

Municipal bonds and tax-free money market accounts can provide attractive, tax-efficient income for those in higher tax brackets.

ACTION STEP: Compare the tax-equivalent yield of tax-free investments with taxable alternatives. Identify where tax-free products could fit in your portfolio.

> EXAMPLE:
> - Caleb allocated a portion of his taxable account to municipal bonds, generating tax-free income that boosted his after-tax returns while reducing exposure to higher tax brackets.

QUESTION: Have you calculated the tax-equivalent yield of tax-free investments compared to taxable alternatives for your situation? Are tax-free investments like municipal bonds or tax-free money markets a good fit for your portfolio? If so, are you utilizing these products effectively in your taxable accounts?

_____

_____

_____

_____

_____

_____

_____

_____

CHAPTER SIX

Advanced Tax Strategies for Optimizing Wealth

In the middle of difficulty lies opportunity.

—ALBERT EINSTEIN

A s we venture deeper into the realm of tax optimization for two-comma wealth, we move from the foundational strategies discussed in the previous chapter to more sophisticated approaches. While understanding tax brackets and basic asset location is crucial, true mastery of wealth preservation demands a more nuanced toolkit. These strategies aren't just about saving money today; they're about optimizing your wealth for the future, ensuring a lasting legacy, and making every dollar work harder for you and your heirs. As Einstein aptly noted, "In the middle of difficulty lies opportunity," and nowhere is this truer than in the complex world of advanced tax planning for high-net-worth individuals.

True mastery of wealth

preservation demands a

more nuanced toolkit.

Gifting Appreciated Stock

If you have appreciated stock in your taxable account, tax-gain harvesting isn't the only strategy to consider. Gifting appreciated stock to heirs in a lower tax bracket, donating it to charity, or contributing it to a donor-advised fund (DAF) can also be incredibly tax-efficient moves. Not only do these strategies allow you to avoid capital gains taxes, but they also provide immediate tax benefits and can support your legacy goals. As I often tell clients—friends don't let friends give cash when they have appreciated stock to give instead! If you're charitably inclined or looking to benefit your heirs, these gifting strategies can make a big difference.

We'll dive deeper into these options in chapter 7, where we'll explore how charitable giving, including setting up a DAF, can maximize your impact while minimizing your tax bill. Whether you're looking to support causes you care about or create a tax-efficient way to transfer wealth to the next generation, these strategies can help you navigate the toll roads of taxable accounts with ease.

Direct Indexing, Concentrated Stock Positions, and Avoiding Wash Sale Pitfalls

For those who have achieved two-comma wealth, direct indexing—owning individual stocks that mirror an index—offers more tax efficiency and customization than traditional index funds and mutual funds. By owning the individual stocks directly, you can take advantage of tax strategies like harvesting gains or losses on your own terms rather than being subject to a fund's internal trades, which can trigger unexpected capital gains. This extra level of control makes direct indexing a powerful tool for managing taxes while keeping your portfolio aligned with your financial goals.

Another big benefit of direct indexing is the ability to personalize your investments. Want to avoid industries that don't align with your personal values or beliefs? Maybe you've had a bad experience with the local XYZ chain and would rather not own a piece of it—direct indexing lets you make those choices. However, keep in mind that excluding certain companies or sectors can sometimes come at the cost of performance or diversification, so it's important to weigh the potential impact on your portfolio. That said, this approach gives you the freedom to align your investments with your values—something you may not be able to do with traditional index or mutual funds, where you're stuck with whatever the fund holds.

Direct indexing— owning individual stocks that mirror an index— offers more tax efficiency and customization than traditional index funds and mutual funds.

Even with exclusions, direct indexing allows you to stay broadly diversified by owning a large enough mix of individual stocks across various sectors. This means you can still spread out risk and maintain a balanced portfolio, ensuring you're not putting all your eggs in one basket—even if you've left a few out for personal reasons.

And for those on the other end of the spectrum who may not own mutual funds or ETFs but are instead sitting on too few individual stocks (perhaps from employer company stock that you acquired while working there), there are strategies to help you diversify these concentrated stock positions without triggering significant taxes. For example, if the stock is held in a qualified plan like a 401(k), the net unrealized appreciation (NUA) strategy can allow you to take advantage of favorable capital gains tax rates on the growth rather than ordinary income rates. Additionally, options like collar strategies and exchange funds can help manage risk and spread your exposure, allowing you to protect and grow your wealth while staying true to your long-term goals. By working closely with a financial advisor, you can explore these strategies and others that may be a good fit for your specific situation.

But while we don't want all our eggs in one basket, we do want to keep all our baskets on the same farm—or, in this case, with the same firm! Consolidating assets with a trusted financial advisor who can see the whole picture ensures that your investments are coordinated and aligned. This approach can also help you avoid common tax pitfalls, like the wash sale rule. The wash sale rule comes into play when you sell a security at a loss and repurchase a substantially identical security within thirty days before or after the sale. Investors often trigger this rule by mistake, perhaps buying the same stock in another account—sometimes in a different type of account, like an IRA where taxes aren't top of mind—or reinvesting dividends in that same stock at another firm while trying to harvest a tax loss elsewhere. When this happens, the IRS disallows the loss, wiping out the benefits of your tax-loss harvesting. Consolidating your baskets of assets with a good financial advisor can help ensure your transactions are coordinated across all accounts, preventing you from inadvertently triggering a wash sale and ensuring your tax strategies work as intended.

> *Consolidating assets with a trusted financial advisor who can see the whole picture ensures that your investments are coordinated and aligned.*

RMDs, Roth Conversions, and QCD

When you hit age seventy-three, the IRS starts requiring you to take required minimum distributions (RMDs) from your tax-deferred accounts, like traditional IRAs, 401(k)s, and the like. These withdrawals are treated as ordinary income, and depending on the size of your accounts, they can easily push you into a higher tax bracket, increasing your tax burden. It's like being forced to take an exit on the toll road even when you're not ready.

One smart move to manage this is converting some of your tax-deferred accounts into a Roth IRA before RMDs kick in. Sure, you'll pay taxes on the conversion upfront, but the long-term benefits—tax-free growth and no RMDs from the Roth—can make it well worth it. It's a matter of balancing a short-term tax hit for future tax freedom. Some people mistakenly think, *I'll just convert my RMD to a Roth when the time comes.* While that sounds great in theory, it doesn't quite work like that. Roth conversions aren't treated as distributions, so they don't count toward your Required Minimum Distribution (RMD) for the year. You'll still need to take your RMD first and pay any taxes due on it, and then, if you want, you can convert additional traditional IRA funds to a Roth—but the RMD itself has to come out as a taxable distribution.

Now, if you're charitably inclined, there's another great tool to consider: qualified charitable distributions (QCDs). Instead of taking your full RMD and paying taxes on it, you can direct up to $108,000 per year from your IRA straight to a qualified charity (indexed for inflation annually). This not only satisfies your RMD requirement but also reduces your taxable income because the amount gifted to charity isn't taxed. Even better, you don't need to itemize your deductions to benefit from this tax-saving strategy, making it accessible to more taxpayers. It's a win-win—you fulfill your philanthropic goals while keeping Uncle Sam from taking a bigger slice of your pie.

The Ten-Year Distribution Rule for Heirs

Thanks to the SECURE Act, most nonspouse heirs who inherit a traditional IRA or 401(k) must now empty the account within ten years, paying ordinary income tax on the distributions. If your heirs are in a high tax bracket, this forced ten-year distribution can create a heavy tax burden, diminishing the wealth you've built.

With Roth IRAs, heirs are still subject to the ten-year rule, but because withdrawals are tax-free, they avoid the hefty tax bill. This makes Roth conversions especially beneficial for legacy planning if you expect your heirs to be in a higher tax bracket than you are.

The Art of Topping Off Tax Brackets

When it comes to Roth conversions, there's an extra layer of strategy you can use to save even more on taxes—topping off your current tax bracket. Think of your income as fitting into buckets. You want to fill up a bucket as much as possible before spilling into the next one because higher tax brackets mean higher taxes. The trick with Roth conversions is to convert just enough each year to stay within a lower tax bracket.

For example, if you're in the 24 percent tax bracket, you can convert enough of your tax-deferred accounts into a Roth to fill that bucket without spilling into the 32 percent bracket. This allows you to convert money at a lower tax rate over several years instead of being hit with a huge tax bill all at once. In lower-income years, like early retirement, you may even be able to stay within the 12 percent tax bracket and pay a very low rate on your conversions.

This "top-off" strategy is especially effective in managing future tax bills. The key is to plan your conversions carefully and to avoid converting so much that you push yourself into a higher tax bracket unnecessarily. A well-executed Roth conversion strategy can help you smooth out your taxable income, avoid big RMDs later, and ultimately pay less in taxes over the long run.

The Widow's Tax
The widow's tax is an often-overlooked risk that occurs when one spouse dies and the surviving spouse is left filing as a single taxpayer.

This change in filing status often pushes the surviving spouse into a higher tax bracket, even though their income may not have changed significantly. This can result in higher taxes on RMDs, Social Security benefits, and other retirement income.

Roth conversions can help mitigate this risk by reducing future taxable income, ensuring that a surviving spouse isn't hit with a much larger tax bill during an already difficult time.

Roth conversions can help mitigate this risk by reducing future taxable income, ensuring that a surviving spouse isn't hit with a much larger tax bill during an already difficult time.

Timing Social Security and Roth Conversions

Everyone wants to know the optimal time to take Social Security. You've probably seen the ads for free steak dinners, promising the "secret" claiming strategy that will unlock piles of extra cash. The truth? Most of the loopholes have been closed. Unless the steak comes with a crystal ball revealing the exact day you'll die, there's no one-size-fits-all strategy. We just don't know the perfect answer. So, assuming you're in good health, let's work with what we can control—your tax efficiency and income planning.

When you retire, your taxable income often drops, and this opens up new routes for Roth conversions and tax efficiency. For example, delaying Social Security can help keep your income low during early retirement, giving you more room to convert traditional IRA or 401(k) assets to Roth IRAs without jumping into a higher tax bracket. The later you delay Social Security (up to age seventy), the larger your monthly benefit grows, so there's an added incentive to postpone it while giving you years of lower income to work with.

By doing this, you'll strategically use the lower-income years to minimize your long-term tax burden while building up tax-free assets in Roth IRAs. Additionally, delaying Social Security keeps your modified adjusted gross income (MAGI) lower, which could help you avoid IRMAA surcharges on Medicare, which we can now get into.

Watch Out for IRMAA (for Medicare Recipients)

When using strategies like Roth conversions, be mindful of IRMAA (income-related monthly adjustment amount), which applies to Medicare recipients. Though the figures change annually, in 2025, if your modified adjusted gross income (MAGI) exceeds $106,000 for single filers or $212,000 for couples, you'll face higher Medicare Part B and Part D premiums. Note: IRMAA is based on your income from two years prior, meaning decisions made in 2025 will impact your Medicare premiums in 2027.

IRMAA increases are tiered, with higher income levels triggering progressively larger premium adjustments up to a maximum. For 2025 MAGI, the highest tier applies to individuals earning more than $500,000 or joint filers earning more than $750,000, where premiums can increase by over $500 per month per person. While no one likes being surprised by extra costs, especially when the bill is from the government, this is where strategic planning becomes essential.

In some cases, it may make sense to be aggressive with Roth conversions in the early years of retirement, even if this means temporarily landing in a higher IRMAA bracket. Doing so can reduce your required minimum distributions (RMDs) later, potentially keeping you out of a lower but consistent IRMAA bracket for life. This kind of strategy highlights the importance of sitting down with an advisor to forecast different scenarios and evaluate your options. We all have a tax tolerance, and understanding yours before implementing strategies—not two years too late—is critical to staying in control of both your tax and health-care costs.

While topping off tax brackets can still be a smart way to manage taxes, even when entering IRMAA brackets, carefully considering these factors ensures that your Roth conversion strategy aligns with your broader financial and retirement goals.

A recent client experience vividly illustrates the importance of considering IRMAA implications before making large financial moves, even when they don't involve Roth conversions. This client, whose wealth was largely tied up in her 401(k), decided to independently roll over her account. To cover the down payment on a $50,000 car, she withdrew $35,000 on her own before rolling over the rest of her 401(k), financing the remaining $15,000 to align with her desired monthly budget. However, this withdrawal, subject to 20 percent withholding, ended up totaling $43,750, pushing her into the IRMAA penalty bracket. Want to hear the worst part, though? The car loan had a zero percent promotional interest rate! Had I been consulted, I would have advised her to finance the full amount and distribute payments from her IRA over time. This approach would have stretched out the taxation, avoided any IRMAA penalties, and kept her budget intact.

Fortunately, by using the sixty-day rollover rule—a special exception that can be used once per year when transferring between IRAs, 401(k)s, and similar accounts—I was able to help mitigate the situation. We rolled other funds back into her IRA, effectively reducing her taxable income and eliminating the IRMAA impact. The lesson here is not just to have a good financial advisor but to consult them before making major purchases or financial moves. They might spot a blind spot you weren't aware of, saving you from the toll of unnecessary taxation.

Balancing RMDs, Roth conversions, QCDs, and these tax-bracket-topping strategies can optimize your retirement plan. Working with a knowledgeable advisor ensures you're

The lesson here is not just to have a good financial advisor but to consult them before making major purchases or financial moves.

navigating these moves at the right times and maximizing your tax efficiency—keeping more of your wealth working for you while avoiding costly mistakes.

Smart Navigation Saves Money

Taxes are the tolls of wealth—inevitable perhaps, but with the right strategies mapped out, you can minimize how much the journey costs you based on the roads you take and when and where you take them. Whether it's through Roth conversions, tax-gain-or-loss harvesting, donor-advised funds, proper asset location, or other tailored strategies, being proactive with your tax planning means you get to keep more of what you've worked so hard to earn. The goal is simple: preserve and grow your wealth while paying no more than your fair share to Uncle Sam.

Protecting your legacy and ensuring that your wealth is passed on smoothly is the next critical step.

But remember, your financial journey doesn't end with minimizing taxes during your lifetime. Protecting your legacy and ensuring that your wealth is passed on smoothly is the next critical step. That's where estate planning comes into play. Just as there are ways to reduce taxes while you're alive, there are strategies to ensure your estate avoids unnecessary taxes after you're gone. In chapter 7, we'll dive deep into estate planning—discussing gifting strategies, trusts, and how to ensure your legacy endures.

SWIM Lesson 6

SWIM Lesson: Master Gifting Strategies

Gifting appreciated stock to heirs or charities can provide significant tax benefits, including avoiding capital gains taxes and aligning with your wealth transfer or philanthropic goals.

ACTION STEP: Review your taxable accounts to identify appreciated assets that could be gifted to heirs in lower tax brackets or donated to charity for tax-efficient wealth transfer or giving.

EXAMPLE
- *Situation:* Jane gifted appreciated stock worth $150,000 with a $50,000 cost basis to her alma mater's endowment fund.
- *Result:* She avoided $15,000 in capital gains taxes while receiving an immediate charitable tax deduction and supporting the school she deeply cares about.

QUESTION: How might gifting appreciated assets align with your wealth transfer goals or philanthropic objectives while optimizing your tax situation?

_____

_____

_____

_____

_____

⊕ SWIM Lesson:
Optimize Roth Conversions and RMD
Management

Strategic Roth conversions before RMDs kick in can lead to long-term tax benefits, especially when using the "top-off" tax bracket strategy to manage taxable income.

ACTION STEP: Review your income so far this year and estimate how much room remains in your current tax bracket. Take one small step, such as withdrawing from a tax-deferred account or converting a portion of your traditional IRA to a Roth IRA, to optimize your tax position before year-end.

> EXAMPLE
> - *Situation:* Steve realized he was $20,000 below the top of the 24 percent tax bracket.
> - *Action:* He converted $15,000 from his traditional IRA to a Roth IRA to maximize his tax efficiency without spilling into a higher bracket.

QUESTION: Have you developed a multi-year plan for Roth conversions that balances current tax costs with future tax savings and accounts for future RMDs?

_____

_____

_____

_____

_____

_____

_____

⊕ SWIM Lesson: Leverage Qualified Charitable Distributions (QCDs)

QCDs can satisfy RMD requirements while reducing taxable income for charitably inclined individuals.

ACTION STEP: If you're over age seventy and a half, explore how directing a portion of your RMDs to charity through QCDs could lower your taxable income and fulfill your giving priorities.

> EXAMPLE
> - *Situation:* Susan wanted to support her local animal shelter.
> - *Action:* She directed $50,000 of her RMD as a QCD, reducing her taxable income while fulfilling her philanthropic goals.

QUESTION: How could QCDs help you meet your charitable goals while minimizing taxable income?

_____

_____

_____

_____

_____

_____

_____

_____

_____

⊕ SWIM Lesson:
Coordinate Social Security Timing with Tax Strategy

Delaying Social Security can create opportunities for tax-efficient Roth conversions and help manage future tax brackets.

ACTION STEP: Evaluate the benefits of delaying Social Security to maximize your monthly benefits and reduce taxable income in early retirement years, freeing up room for Roth conversions.

> EXAMPLE
> - *Action:* Alex delayed Social Security until age seventy, using the lower-income years to complete Roth conversions.
> - *Result:* This strategy minimized his future RMDs and increased his tax-free income from Roth accounts.

QUESTION: How does your planned Social Security claiming age align with your overall tax strategy and retirement goals?

_____

_____

_____

_____

_____

_____

_____

_____

_____

⊕ SWIM Lesson:
Navigate IRMAA and Plan for the "Widow's Tax"

Be mindful of income-related monthly adjustment amount (IRMAA) thresholds and potential changes in filing status, like becoming a surviving spouse.

ACTION STEP: Work with your financial advisor to structure your income and Roth conversions to avoid IRMAA surcharges and mitigate the impact of the widow's tax on future filings.

EXAMPLE
- *Situation:* Joe, who is eight years older than his wife Karen, is worried about future tax rates.
- *Action:* Joe and Karen work with their advisors to pre-emptively implement Roth conversions earlier on in order to reduce future RMDs, keeping Karen's future taxes lower and avoiding IRMAA penalties.

QUESTION: What steps can you take now to avoid Medicare surcharges and manage the potential tax implications of filing as a single taxpayer in the future?

_____

_____

_____

_____

_____

_____

_____

CHAPTER SEVEN
Fortifying Your Financial Legacy

Only put off until tomorrow what you are
willing to die having left undone.

—PABLO PICASSO

I t's not the most pleasant topic, but planning for what happens after you're gone is one of the most valuable things you can do for your loved ones. For those with two-comma wealth, it's especially important to consider how to protect and preserve the assets you've built. Without an estate plan in place, you might be leaving it up to the government or courts to decide—and let's just say their idea of an "efficient" transfer probably doesn't match yours. Taking control of your estate plan ensures that your hard-earned wealth is distributed according to your wishes and not left to the red tape and the very public nature of bureaucracy.

Estate planning isn't just about taxes and paperwork—it's about ensuring that your wealth serves its purpose and reflects your values.

Estate planning isn't just about taxes and paperwork—it's about ensuring that your wealth serves its purpose and reflects your values.

Whether it's passing wealth to your heirs, supporting your favorite charities, or protecting your legacy from unnecessary legal and tax burdens, the goal is to create a plan that works for you and your loved ones. Without it, your heirs might face unnecessary conflict, excessive taxes, and costly probate processes.

Keeping the Peace when Wealth Is Involved

Money can change people, and that can create tension, especially when inheritance is at stake. In-laws can become outlaws, and even the closest siblings can turn on each other. If you have a significant amount of wealth, those dynamics can become even more complex.

Take, for example, a family with three children. One child has been receiving financial help over the years due to life circumstances, while the other two have not needed anything so far. You want to treat your kids fairly, but how do you do that when their financial needs are so different?

A great way to approach this is by setting up separate brokerage accounts in your name with transfer-on-death (TOD) designations for the two children who don't need help right now. As you give money to the third child, you can deposit equal amounts into those accounts for the other two. This allows you to ensure each child is treated fairly without gifting large sums immediately. When you pass away, the assets in the TOD accounts transfer directly to the named beneficiaries with a step-up in basis, meaning their tax burden will be minimized.

If estate taxes are a concern, taking advantage of the annual gift tax exclusion—which is $19,000 per person in 2025 (meaning you can give twice that amount if you are married)—lets you give to your kids (and their spouses, children or anyone else) tax-free, reducing your taxable estate over time. If your kids happen to be in a lower tax bracket than you and you have stock that has appreciated in value, giving them stock can be more efficient than selling the stock and giving cash. This strategy not only helps equalize gifts but also gives you peace of mind, knowing your kids are treated fairly while keeping everything organized and efficient.

Family Harmony

One of my clients faced a situation that perfectly illustrates just how complex estate planning can be when family dynamics are involved. Over the years, they had accumulated several real estate properties, and one of their children had partnered with them on a few, purchasing a 50 percent stake. When it came time to plan the estate, the client intended to divide all the properties evenly between their children. However, the child who co-owned the properties felt they should fully inherit the ones they had partnered on. The other sibling, on the other hand, believed they should receive half of the parent's 50 percent share in those co-owned properties.

Typically, in cases like this, after the death of the parents, a valuation would be conducted to determine the fair market value of the properties, and one sibling would buy out the other of their share— often by getting a loan or using other assets to make it happen. But in this case, that solution wasn't acceptable to the child who had been a partner in the properties. The co-owner felt that being forced to buy out their sibling's share of something they had worked on for years was unfair. On the other hand, the other sibling didn't see why they should walk away with less of the estate, especially since their parents had always talked about dividing everything equally.

It was a challenging situation. Emotions were high, and both siblings felt strongly about their perspectives. The parents wanted to find a resolution that wouldn't fracture the family but also wanted to honor the hard work and partnership that had gone into the properties.

In the end, they worked through it by conducting a current valuation of all the properties in the estate at the time the estate planning was executed. The co-owning sibling received full ownership of the properties they had partnered on, while the other sibling received a larger share of other assets to balance the total value. It wasn't a perfect solution, but it allowed the family to maintain harmony, and both siblings felt respected in the process.

This story highlights the importance of flexibility and communication in estate planning. What looks "equal" on paper might not always feel fair to everyone involved. In this case, avoiding a forced buyout and instead restructuring the division of assets allowed everyone to move forward with their relationships intact. And sometimes, that's what estate planning is really about—finding a solution that works for the whole family, even if it requires some creative thinking.

What looks "equal" on paper might not always feel fair to everyone involved.

The key takeaway is that communication is essential. Having open discussions about your estate plans with your heirs, guided by your financial advisor and attorney ahead of time, can prevent misunderstandings and help maintain family unity. Family meetings facilitated by a professional team of financial and legal advisors can help ensure that everyone understands your wishes and the work that went into building your two-comma wealth, making them feel responsible for managing it well rather than viewing it as a windfall.

Avoiding Probate

If you've ever been through probate, you already know it's not something you want your heirs to endure. Probate is a court-supervised process where a will is validated and your assets are distributed. It can be time-consuming, expensive, and, as I already mentioned, very public. Your family might be forced to wait months—sometimes years—to access what you've left them, all while paying attorney fees and dealing with administrative headaches.

One of the key goals in estate planning should be to avoid probate whenever possible. You can accomplish this through tools such as transfer-on-death (TOD) accounts, Lady Bird deeds for real estate (available in states like Florida, Texas, and Michigan), and revocable living trusts. These tools allow your assets to pass directly to your heirs, bypassing the courts, saving time and money, and keeping your financial matters private.

One of the key goals in estate planning should be to avoid probate whenever possible.

Proper estate planning can help you maintain privacy and avoid the significant delays and costs associated with the probate process.

Health Savings Accounts: Turning a Tax Bomb into a Legacy Tool

As part of streamlining and protecting your financial legacy, it's essential to address specific assets that require special consideration in estate planning. Health savings accounts (HSAs), celebrated for their triple tax-free advantage—tax-deductible contributions, tax-free growth, and tax-free withdrawals (see chapter 5)—are among the most powerful tools available during your lifetime. However, without careful planning, they can create unintended challenges for your heirs.

Unlike IRAs, which offer a ten-year stretch period for beneficiaries, nonspouse heirs of HSAs are required to take the entire account balance as taxable income in the year they inherit it. This creates an immediate and often substantial tax liability, especially for high-income heirs. While a surviving spouse can inherit an HSA and treat it as their own, maintaining all its tax benefits, the lack of stretch provisions for other heirs makes proactive planning even more critical.

One effective strategy is to name a charity as the contingent beneficiary of your HSA. Charities, being tax-exempt, can receive the full value of the account without triggering income taxes. This ensures the funds are put to meaningful use without creating a financial burden for your heirs. This strategy works particularly well for any remaining HSA balance after the death of a second spouse, where the account might otherwise become a taxable windfall for nonspouse beneficiaries.

Alternatively, you can reduce the account balance strategically during your lifetime by reimbursing yourself for any unreimbursed medical expenses. Revisiting saved receipts allows you to withdraw these funds tax-free and reinvest them into a taxable account. Once in a taxable account, the assets receive a step-up in basis upon your passing, significantly reducing the tax impact for your heirs while preserving more of your wealth.

If charity isn't a priority, rolling unused HSA funds into a traditional IRA before the death of the second spouse is another viable strategy. While this doesn't eliminate the tax burden, it does allow heirs to stretch distributions over ten years rather than taking the full amount in a single year, easing the immediate impact.

As HSAs grow in popularity and contribution limits rise to match increasing health-care costs, these accounts are expected to hold even greater value for two-comma wealth families. This is a double-edged sword. While larger balances enhance their potential for tax-free growth and spending flexibility, they also amplify the tax challenges for heirs if not managed effectively.

Proactively managing your HSA isn't just about avoiding pitfalls. It's about maximizing the account's potential as a multigenerational tool that supports your family's financial goals. By working with a financial advisor, you can ensure these accounts are integrated seamlessly into your estate plan. Additionally, educating younger generations on the strategic use of HSAs for accumulation and older generations on proper distribution techniques creates a unified family approach to managing these accounts.

When addressed thoughtfully, HSAs can evolve from a potential tax bomb into a legacy tool. Whether supporting a favorite cause, funding health care in retirement, or simplifying wealth transfer for your heirs, these accounts are a key element in fortifying your financial legacy.

Consolidation: Simplifying the Inheritance Process

Whether it's HSAs, IRAs, Roths, 401(k)s, or any of a plethora of other accounts, it's not uncommon for people to accumulate a sprawling array of financial accounts over their lifetime. While some of these accounts are required due to the tax code, I often find that people have multiple accounts of the same type but held at several different institutions. Though this may seem like a way to diversify, it can quickly become a logistical nightmare for heirs when the time comes to settle your estate. I once had a client whose assets were spread across more than thirty financial institutions. The executor—the client's oldest adult child—was overwhelmed as they scrambled to track down every account, from life insurance policies and IRAs to 401(k)s, CDs, and brokerage accounts.

The process took months, filled with frustration, delays, and additional expenses. This stress came at a time when they were already grieving the loss of a loved one. Unfortunately, this scenario is all too common. Many people keep their accounts scattered because they fear putting all their eggs in one basket. However, with modern full-service brokerage firms, this concern is largely outdated.

It's not about having all your eggs in one basket—it's about keeping them on one farm.

It's not about having all

your eggs in one basket—

it's about keeping

them on one farm.

As we discussed in chapter 6, consolidating accounts under one trusted institution or advisor, you can achieve diversification within your portfolio while dramatically simplifying management. This approach not only ensures better oversight during your lifetime but also prevents your heirs from enduring a scavenger hunt to find what you've left behind. Consolidation isn't just a convenience—it's a practical way to reduce unnecessary stress during an already emotional time.

Moreover, having all your accounts in one place during your lifetime helps you avoid potential pitfalls such as wash sale violations during tax-loss harvesting or unintentional overconcentration through overlapping investments—the very issue people try to avoid by scattering their assets. Consolidating accounts allows for comprehensive portfolio management, ensuring proper diversification and alignment with your financial goals.

Whether for your peace of mind or to reduce the burden on your heirs, consolidating accounts is a foundational step in creating a well-organized estate plan. When paired with strategies like trusts and clear beneficiary designations, it ensures your two-comma wealth is managed efficiently, protected, and passed on as you intend.

Trusts

Trusts can be one of the most effective tools for keeping your wealth protected and your wishes respected. They help guard against family conflicts, potential divorces, and those unpredictable curveballs life tends to throw. Trusts are about creating a thoughtful plan for how and when your assets will be distributed, ensuring they're handled responsibly and in line with your wishes.

Here's a scenario I've seen more times than I'd like to admit: A child inherits their share of the family wealth, then goes through a divorce, and suddenly half of that inheritance could end up with their ex-spouse. I like to call this situation the moment an in-law becomes an out-law. A well-structured trust can stop this in its tracks, keeping what's meant for your heirs right where it belongs.

Even if you're the one inheriting wealth later in life, it's important to protect it. Gray divorces, those that happen after decades of marriage, are increasingly common. Keeping inherited assets separate from marital property by avoiding commingling can make all the difference. For those less familiar, commingling occurs when inherited funds or property are mixed with joint accounts or used to purchase joint assets, making it harder to claim them as separate property during a divorce.

Trusts can also help if you have a family business and need to balance the scales between kids who are involved in the business and those who aren't. They're equally useful for ensuring that wealth is distributed equitably while avoiding unnecessary conflicts.

Trusts let you create a fair and thoughtful plan that works for every member of your family while avoiding unnecessary conflicts.

One of the most attractive benefits of trusts is their ability to help your estate avoid probate, saving time, money, and stress for your heirs. Probate can be costly and, worse, a public process, exposing your financial matters to anyone who cares to look. Trusts keep these details private, ensuring that the administration of your estate remains discreet. They also provide a level of asset protection in certain cases, shielding wealth from creditors or legal claims.

But it's not enough to simply draft a trust and call it a day. Funding the trust—transferring

Trusts let you create a fair and thoughtful plan that works for every member of your family while avoiding unnecessary conflicts.

and retitling assets to ensure they're owned by the trust—is just as important. I've seen too many clients proudly show me a beautifully bound trust document they paid thousands of dollars for, only to discover they never funded it. Without proper funding, that expensive binder might as well have come from the office supply store. This underscores the importance of working with a trusted financial advisor who can quarterback the process, ensuring your assets, estate planning attorney, and CPA are all aligned and working together.

Estate Taxes and Trust Strategies

Ben Franklin famously remarked, "In this world, nothing is certain except death and taxes." Estate taxes combine these two certainties in a way that can feel like Uncle Sam's last laugh. Fortunately, with careful planning, you can ensure that your wealth is preserved for your loved ones and doesn't become an unexpected windfall for the taxman.

The potential impact of estate taxes is significant. In 2025, the federal estate tax exemption is $13.99 million, but in 2026, it is scheduled to significantly decrease unless a new law is enacted. This scheduled change will subject more estates to a 40 percent federal tax rate. For those living in states with their own estate or inheritance taxes, such as New York, Maryland, or New Jersey, the burden can be even greater. These states often have lower thresholds or impose inheritance taxes based on who receives the assets. For example, New Jersey's inheritance tax threshold for certain beneficiaries is as low as $25,000, while Kentucky taxes some heirs after just $1,000. Oregon has an estate tax exemption of only $1 million, one of the lowest in the country.

Many states exempt immediate family members like spouses and children from these taxes, but the rules vary significantly depending on the amount inherited and the relationship of the recipient to the deceased. Understanding these nuances is critical, especially for two-comma wealth families who might cross these thresholds as their wealth grows.

Types of Trusts

Trusts are like a Swiss Army knife for your estate plan—there's a version to address just about any financial goal. Here's a rundown of some of the most popular trust options and what they can do for you:

- GRANTOR-RETAINED ANNUITY TRUSTS (GRATS): Think of GRATs as a way to transfer appreciating assets to your heirs without getting slammed with gift taxes. You get annual payments for a set term, and the remaining assets go to your beneficiaries, all while keeping things tax-efficient.
- IRREVOCABLE LIFE INSURANCE TRUSTS (ILITS): These trusts are designed to hold life insurance policies outside your taxable estate. They help reduce estate taxes and give your heirs the liquidity they need to cover taxes or other expenses.
- REVOCABLE LIVING TRUSTS: If avoiding probate and keeping things private are priorities for you, this is the way to go. These trusts make it easier to transfer assets to your heirs while ensuring your estate stays out of public records.
- CHARITABLE REMAINDER TRUSTS (CRTS): Want to give back and get a tax break at the same time? CRTs let you receive income during your lifetime, provide a tax deduction, and leave what's left to charity.
- CHARITABLE LEAD TRUSTS (CLTS): These trusts let you support a cause you care about while keeping things tax-efficient. They provide income to a charity for a set period, and the remaining assets go to your heirs, reducing your taxable estate in the process.

- QUALIFIED PERSONAL RESIDENCE TRUSTS (QPRTS): These are perfect if you want to transfer your home to your heirs while still living there for a set period. They help lower the home's value for estate tax purposes, saving your family money in the long run.
- SPOUSAL LIFETIME ACCESS TRUSTS (SLATS): SLATs are a great option for married couples. They remove assets from your estate while letting your spouse access income or distributions, giving you flexibility and tax savings.
- DYNASTY TRUSTS: These are for long-term planners. They protect assets from estate taxes, creditors, and divorces, ensuring your wealth benefits multiple generations.
- TRUSTS FOR BLENDED FAMILIES (QTIP TRUSTS): These are a lifesaver for blended families. They make sure your surviving spouse is cared for while protecting assets for children from a previous marriage.

Each of these trusts serves a specific purpose, whether it's reducing taxes, managing family dynamics, or creating a long-term wealth plan.

Power of Attorney

A durable power of attorney (POA) is one of the most important tools in your estate plan. This document allows someone you trust to manage your financial affairs if you become incapacitated. Without a POA in place, your family might have to go through a court process to get a guardian appointed who may or may not be someone you want and all the administrative headaches that go with this process. This can be an emotionally draining experience, especially during a crisis.

Even for married couples, it's critical to understand that some of your largest accounts—like IRAs—cannot be titled in joint names. Now, imagine the unthinkable: a sudden health event or serious accident leaves your spouse incapacitated and unable to manage their affairs. Think back to the COVID-19 pandemic, when the possibility of loved ones being placed on ventilators was a harsh reality for many families. Without a properly executed durable power of attorney (POA), not only would you be unable to access these accounts, but financial institutions—and even your trusted financial advisor—would be legally prohibited from discussing them with you, regardless of how closely you've been involved in planning together over the years.

It's a scenario no one wants to face, especially during an already emotional and stressful time. Fortunately, it's also entirely avoidable. A durable POA ensures that you can act on your spouse's behalf if the unexpected happens, providing the authority to manage financial accounts, access funds, and make necessary decisions. Proper planning today can save you from unnecessary complications and give you peace of mind for whatever the future may bring.

Equally important is having a health-care power of attorney and a living will or advance directive. These documents ensure that your health-care decisions are carried out according to your wishes and prevent family disagreements during emotionally charged times. I've seen families torn apart by disagreements over end-of-life care, which could have been avoided with proper documentation.

Charitable Giving

Giving to charity isn't just a powerful way to leave a lasting legacy—it's also a smart tax strategy, especially for those with two-comma wealth. The goal isn't just to give but to give in the most tax-efficient way possible so your contributions have the biggest impact on both your charitable causes and your wealth preservation.

Being Intentional with Your Charitable Legacy

In the United States, tipping has become an unavoidable part of life—and lately, it feels like it's gotten a bit out of hand. From your morning coffee run to picking up takeout, those little screens pop up, nudging you to leave 15 percent, 20 percent, or even 30 percent before you've even received your order. What was once a way to show appreciation for exceptional service has started to feel like an obligation—and sometimes, it's hard to tell if the intent behind tipping is still about rewarding those who deserve it.

When it comes to your financial legacy, however, you have the chance to be thoughtful and deliberate. With a little planning, you can "tip" the causes and charities that matter most to you while maximizing what's left for your loved ones. And here's the kicker: By structuring your giving wisely, you can ensure Uncle Sam doesn't end up getting more than his fair share. We want to pay the taxes we owe, but there's no requirement to leave a tip.

Let's illustrate this with an example. Say you want to leave 10 percent of your estate to a charity and the rest to your children. You're all in the 32 percent tax bracket, and your assets include the following:

- *$1 million in a traditional IRA* (tax-deferred)
- *$1 million in a Roth IRA* (tax-free)
- *$1 million in a brokerage account* (eligible for a step-up in basis upon your passing)

If you leave 10 percent of the estate to charity as a percentage of the total, here's what happens:

1. *The charity receives $300,000* (10 percent of the total estate).
2. *Your children inherit the rest.* However, note the following:
   - The $900,000 from the traditional IRA will eventually be taxed as ordinary income when they withdraw it.

- The $900,000 from the Roth IRA remains tax-free.
- The $900,000 in the brokerage account benefits from a step-up in basis, making it more tax-efficient.

This approach works, but here's how to make it better:

A Smarter Way to Structure It

Instead of leaving 10 percent of everything to charity, designate the *$300,000 directly from the traditional IRA* to the charity. Here's why this is a win-win:

- Charities are tax-exempt, so they can receive 100 percent of the donation from the IRA with no tax consequences.
- This leaves the *Roth IRA* and the *brokerage account* for your children, maximizing their inheritance in a tax-efficient way:
  - They still get the $1,00,000 from the Roth IRA tax-free.
  - They inherit the brokerage account with a stepped-up basis, avoiding capital gains taxes on the appreciated value.

In this scenario, your children inherit more wealth while the charity still receives the full donation. Let's break down the numbers:

Original Scenario
- Charity: $300,000
- Children
  - $900,000 from the traditional IRA (taxable, effectively worth $612,000 after 32 percent taxes).
  - $900,000 from the Roth IRA (tax-free).
  - $900,000 from the brokerage account (step-up basis).
  - *Net for children: $2,412,000.*

Tax-Efficient Scenario
- Charity: $300,000 directly from the traditional IRA.
- Children
  - $1,000,000 from the Roth IRA (tax-free).
  - $1,000,000 from the brokerage account (step-up basis).
  - Remaining $700,000 from the traditional IRA (taxable, worth $476,000 after 32 percent taxes).
  - *Net for children: $2,476,000.*

Your children receive *$64,000 more*, and the charity still receives its full $300,000 donation.

The Takeaway

This simple adjustment ensures you maximize your wealth's impact—both for your family and the causes you care about. It's one of the many ways careful planning can leave everyone in a better position, without accidentally tipping the IRS. While structuring your estate plan and beneficiaries thoughtfully is important, donating to charities during your lifetime often provides both the personal satisfaction of seeing your impact and significant tax benefits that can enhance your giving potential. Let's discuss some of the most effective giving strategies you can implement during your lifetime.

Gifting as a Strategy

Another effective way to reduce your taxable estate is by taking advantage of the annual gift tax exclusion, which allows you to gift $19,000 per person in 2025 without triggering the need to file IRS Form 709. Married couples can double this amount, gifting $38,000 per person. These gifts are a great way to reduce the size of your estate without any tax consequences.

For instance, let's say you have two children, each married, and they each have two children of their own (your grandchildren). As a couple, you and your spouse could gift $38,000 to each of your two children, their spouses, and your four grandchildren. That's a total of $304,000 in tax-free gifts in just one year (and could be done each and every year), significantly reducing the size of your estate without triggering gift taxes.

And if you gift appreciated assets like stocks instead of cash, the benefits can be even greater. If the recipient is in a lower tax bracket, they may pay less in capital gains taxes when they sell the stock than you would. For example, gifting $38,000 of low-basis stock to a child who pays a 0 percent long-term capital gains rate instead of your 20 percent rate can save thousands—just beware of the kiddie tax if they are under age twenty-four.

These gifting strategies don't just help reduce your estate; they also allow you to see the impact of your wealth during your lifetime. Whether it's helping with education, starting a business, or simply easing a loved one's financial burden, gifting offers a meaningful way to create a legacy while minimizing estate tax liabilities.

Qualified Charitable Distributions (QCDs)

As we mentioned in chapter 6, if you're over seventy and a half, one of the most effective ways to give is through qualified charitable distributions (QCDs). These allow you to donate directly from your IRA, meeting your required minimum distributions (RMDs) while avoiding the taxes you would normally owe on those withdrawals. It's like hitting two birds with one stone: You support causes that matter to you while lowering your taxable income. For those with significant wealth in traditional IRA and 401(k) accounts, using a QCD can help manage the size of your RMDs, which could otherwise push you into a higher tax bracket.

Donor-Advised Funds (DAFs)

For those with two-comma wealth, where charitable giving plays a big role in financial planning, donor-advised funds (DAFs) are a perfect vehicle for maximizing both your impact and your tax savings. A DAF allows you to make a large donation in a single year, giving you a sizable tax deduction right away. But here's the best part: You don't have to decide which charities to support all at once. You can distribute the funds over several years, giving you flexibility while still locking in the tax benefit now.

Why Fund Your DAF with Appreciated Stock?

If you're in the two-comma wealth category, chances are you have appreciated assets in your portfolio—stocks, mutual funds, or other investments that have significantly increased in value. Instead of donating cash, consider contributing these appreciated assets to your DAF. By doing so, you avoid paying capital gains taxes on the growth, and you get to deduct the full fair market value of the stock at the time of the donation (subject to annual limits). For example, if you bought stock years ago for $50,000 and it's now worth $150,000, donating it directly to your DAF lets you bypass capital gains tax on the $100,000 gain and still take a $150,000 deduction. This strategy significantly reduces your taxable income and ensures that more of your wealth goes toward charitable causes rather than taxes. As mentioned in chapter 6—friends don't let friends donate unappreciated assets.

Bunching Donations

Here's another smart strategy for two-comma wealth individuals: bunching donations. Instead of spreading your charitable contributions evenly over several years, consider bunching them into one tax year to take full advantage of the tax benefits. For instance, if you normally give $15,000 each year to charity, you could contribute $45,000 or more to a donor-advised fund in a single year. This may allow you to exceed the standard deduction threshold and take a larger charitable deduction in one year while still distributing the funds to charities over the next few years. At the very least, you could simply give two years' worth of donations at the end of a year to help get you over the limit. This is particularly useful for those whose charitable donations might not be large enough to surpass the standard deduction each year. By bunching donations, you maximize your deductions in high-income years, lowering your tax bill while supporting the causes you care about.

Why Generosity Is a Win-Win for Two-Comma Wealth

For individuals with two-comma wealth, it's about striking the right balance between generosity and tax efficiency. Whether you're using QCDs to lower your RMDs and taxable income, funding a DAF with appreciated stock to avoid capital gains, or bunching donations for maximum tax impact, each of these strategies helps you make the most of your wealth. Plus, you get the satisfaction of seeing the impact of your charitable giving during your lifetime while reducing the size of your taxable estate—ultimately benefiting both your heirs and the causes you care about most.

Giving is a way to not only support causes you care about but also to leverage financial strategies that maximize the impact of your generosity while safeguarding your financial legacy for future generations.

Giving is a way to not only support causes you care about but also to leverage financial strategies that maximize the impact of your generosity while safeguarding your financial legacy for future generations.

Protecting Your Wealth:
Asset Titling, Liability, and Digital Legacy

When it comes to safeguarding your wealth, the way you structure your assets plays a significant role in shielding them from creditors, lawsuits, and other unforeseen challenges. From proper titling to strategic use of trusts, there are tools available to help ensure your financial legacy is both secure and accessible for future generations.

Asset Titling and Creditor Protection

How you title your assets can determine whether they bypass probate, stay protected from creditors, or both. For married couples, tenancy by the entireties (TBE) is one of the most effective ways to safeguard jointly held property. Available in states like Florida, Delaware, and Maryland, TBE treats both spouses as a single legal entity. This means that creditors cannot claim property titled as TBE unless both spouses owe the debt.

As someone based in Florida—a state where many two-comma wealth families relocate to enjoy the weather and tax advantages—I often see clients who don't realize TBE is an option. Many come from states where TBE isn't available, and they default to titling assets as joint tenancy with rights of survivorship (JTWROS), which doesn't offer the same level of creditor protection. Updating your account titling to TBE can typically be done through your bank or financial institution, and it is a simple yet powerful way to shield marital assets.

When it comes to individual accounts, however, I often encounter well-meaning parents who add an adult child to their checking account to help with bill payments or make inheritance easier upon their passing. While it may seem like a convenient solution, it's completely the wrong way to handle it and can lead to unintended legal, financial, and tax consequences.

Why Adding a Child to an Account Is Problematic

1. Adding a child makes them a co-owner of the account, which means their creditors can pursue it. For example, if the child gets into a car accident and is sued, the account could be at risk.
2. It could be considered a partial gift of the account, requiring you to file a gift tax return. If the gift exceeds the annual exclusion limit ($19,000 per recipient in 2025), it reduces your lifetime gift and estate tax exemption, complicating your tax situation.
3. If you add one child under the assumption they'll "distribute" the funds after your passing, it bypasses the estate or TOD (transfer on death) process. This can lead to disputes among siblings and tax issues, as the added child legally owns the account and is under no obligation to share, which then forces them to deal with gift tax laws if they do share.
4. If the account holds appreciated assets like investments, the child's ownership might disrupt the step-up in cost basis upon your passing. This could result in significant capital gains taxes for your heirs.
5. By making your child a co-owner, you're giving them access to the account, which could lead to misuse, intentional or not, or unnecessary complications.

How to Handle It Correctly

1. To pay bills, grant your child a power of attorney (POA). This allows them to manage your account for specific purposes without making them a legal co-owner.
2. To ensure smooth inheritance, use TOD (transfer on death) or POD (payable on death) designations. This ensures the account bypasses probate and goes directly to your intended beneficiaries upon your death.

3. For comprehensive planning, set up a revocable trust, title the account in the name of the trust, and name your child as successor trustee and beneficiary. This approach ensures smooth management during your lifetime and a seamless transfer after your passing.

Why Proper Titling Matters

Proper asset titling offers several benefits:

- Avoiding probate by using TOD, POD, or trust structures ensures your estate remains private and reduces delays for your heirs.
- Protecting assets from creditors through TBE for married couples or trust structures for individuals shields your wealth while maintaining control.
- Maintaining your estate intentions ensures assets are distributed according to your wishes without unnecessary complications or disputes.

These are some of the most common errors I see when working with new clients, and fixing them is always a top priority. Don't take shortcuts with your estate planning. With a little preparation, you can avoid exposing your assets to unnecessary risks and ensure they're passed on smoothly and efficiently. A proactive approach protects your wealth, your intentions, and your peace of mind.

Liability Protection and the Role of Insurance

Beyond asset titling, liability insurance provides a crucial safety net. Umbrella insurance, for instance, supplements your homeowners and auto policies by covering claims that exceed their limits. Imagine being involved in a car accident with damages exceeding your auto insurance coverage. Without an umbrella policy, you could be forced to pay the difference out of pocket. With this additional coverage, your assets remain protected, offering peace of mind against life's uncertainties.

However, umbrella insurance isn't stand-alone. It works in conjunction with existing policies, so it's essential to ensure your base coverage is sufficient to activate the umbrella's protection. Reviewing these policies with a trusted advisor can help you achieve seamless and comprehensive coverage.

Trusts and Asset Protection

Trusts are another layer of defense for protecting your wealth. While their primary purpose is often to reduce estate taxes or streamline inheritance, certain types of trusts also provide robust creditor protection. Some examples include the following:

- IRREVOCABLE TRUSTS: Once assets are placed in an irrevocable trust, they are no longer considered part of your estate. This protects them from creditors and lawsuits while ensuring they are preserved for your heirs.
- DISCRETIONARY TRUSTS: These give trustees the authority to decide when and how to distribute funds to beneficiaries, making it difficult for creditors to access those assets.
- SPENDTHRIFT TRUSTS: Designed for heirs who may struggle with financial responsibility, these trusts prevent beneficiaries from selling or borrowing against their inheritance, protecting assets from creditors.

For clients who own rental properties or other high-liability assets, combining trusts with a limited liability company (LLC) can create a formidable asset protection strategy. An LLC separates your personal wealth from the property's liabilities, while the trust ensures long-term preservation of those assets. Irrevocable trusts should be considered carefully since, as the name implies, you permanently lose direct control over the assets. These trusts are more complex and costly to maintain and may incur additional tax consequences due to less favorable tax rates.

Safeguarding Your Digital Legacy

Estate planning used to mean just wills, trusts, and property. Today, your legacy includes everything from online banking accounts to social media profiles. Ignoring these digital assets can leave gaps in an otherwise airtight estate plan.

In today's interconnected world, your financial and personal legacy extends far beyond physical assets. A growing portion of your life is stored digitally, and failing to plan for this can lead to confusion and frustration for your heirs. Just as you organize your tangible wealth, taking steps to manage your digital footprint ensures a smooth transition for those settling your estate.

One client shared how her father kept passwords scribbled on scraps of paper—many of them outdated. The family spent weeks trying to access accounts, compounding their grief with unnecessary stress. This all-too-common scenario underscores the importance of planning ahead.

In today's digital age, managing your digital legacy is just as important as your physical assets. Tools like password managers, such as LastPass or Dashlane, simplify the process of securely storing your log-ins and granting emergency access to trusted loved ones when needed. Enabling two-step verification provides an extra layer of security for sensitive accounts.

In chapter 9, we will discuss tips for protecting yourself from digital fraud, including the child-in-distress scam—where fraudsters use AI and public social media details to deceive you. Protecting yourself begins though with safeguarding your digital assets and your personal information to ensure your legacy remains secure.

Planning for Life's Changes

Life changes—so should your estate plan. As your family grows, assets change, and laws evolve, it's crucial to regularly review your will, trust, POAs, and other estate documents. Maybe you forgot to update a beneficiary after a divorce, or maybe you set up a trust but never moved assets into it—these seemingly minor oversights can lead to major problems for your heirs.

As your family grows, assets change, and laws evolve, it's crucial to regularly review your will, trust, POAs, and other estate documents.

An estate plan isn't static; it's a living document that evolves with your circumstances, your family, and the law. Key life events like births, marriages, divorces, or significant asset acquisitions are natural opportunities to revisit your plan. Even without these milestones, a periodic review every three to five years ensures your strategy stays relevant and accounts for changes in tax laws or your financial goals.

With two-comma wealth, you have the power to shape your family's future. A well-thought-out estate plan can minimize taxes, strife, and arguing, transforming your wealth into a blessing for your loved ones rather than a malediction that divides them. Money has the potential to bring families together or drive them apart—the difference lies in thoughtful preparation.

The key is starting early and not leaving your plan to chance. By working with the right team of financial advisors, estate attorneys, and CPAs, you can craft a strategy that aligns with your values and ensures a smooth transition of your assets.

Your estate plan isn't just about wealth; it's about the story your success will tell and the legacy it will leave. The question is, what story will your estate tell?

SWIM Lesson 7

SWIM Lesson:
Estate Planning Is Essential for Preserving Wealth

A well-structured estate plan ensures your wealth is passed on smoothly, minimizing taxes and family conflict.

ACTION STEP: Review your estate plan and verify that all documents—wills, trusts, and POAs—are up to date and reflect your current wishes.

EXAMPLE
- *Situation:* "My will is over ten years old, and I've acquired new assets since then."
- *Action:* "I'll schedule a meeting with my estate attorney this month to update my documents and ensure all assets are accounted for."

QUESTION: Does your estate plan clearly outline how your assets will be distributed and what end-of-life care you prefer? What updates might be needed?

_____

_____

_____

_____

_____

_____

_____

⊕ SWIM Lesson:
Communication Prevents Family Conflict

Open discussions about your estate with family members can help avoid misunderstandings and maintain harmony.

ACTION STEP: Create a simple list of key financial documents (e.g., wills, trusts, account log-ins) and share the secure location information with a trusted family member. Set up a meeting with your financial advisor to introduce them to your family, ensuring they have a trusted point of contact before a crisis arises.

EXAMPLE
- *Situation:* "I want my children to understand my intentions and avoid conflicts after I'm gone."
- *Action:* "I'll compile a list of assets and estate plans, discuss it with my family at our next gathering, and bring in my financial advisor to answer questions."

QUESTION: Have you communicated your estate plans to your heirs? How might sharing your intentions now prevent misunderstandings later?

_____

_____

_____

_____

_____

_____

_____

_____

◉ SWIM Lesson:
Ensure Proper Asset Titling and Updated POAs

Proper titling ensures your assets are protected, transferred efficiently, and reflect your estate intentions, while an updated POA ensures smooth management during unforeseen events.

ACTION STEP: Review all accounts and property titles to confirm they are correctly titled (e.g., TOD/POD designations, trust ownership). Ensure your durable power of attorney (POA) is updated and on file with all financial institutions.

> EXAMPLE
> - *Situation:* "I discovered that my investment account is still titled in my name without a TOD designation."
> - *Action:* "I'll contact my financial institution this week to add a TOD designation and confirm my updated POA is on file."

QUESTION: Are all your assets appropriately titled, and is an updated POA on file with your financial institutions to ensure smooth transitions and management?

_____

_____

_____

_____

_____

_____

_____

⊕ SWIM Lesson:
Trusts Provide Protection and Flexibility

Trusts can shield your assets from legal disputes, divorces, and creditors while ensuring they are distributed responsibly.

ACTION STEP: Work with an estate attorney to establish trusts tailored to your needs, such as irrevocable trusts, SLATs, or QPRTs. Review your umbrella insurance policy to enhance asset protection.

EXAMPLE
- *Situation:* "I want to protect my family business from disputes between heirs."
- *Action:* "I'll consult with my attorney to create a trust that ensures business continuity and fairness among my children."

QUESTION: Have you considered setting up a trust to protect your assets and ensure they are distributed according to your wishes? Are your insurance protections adequate?

_____

_____

_____

_____

_____

_____

_____

⊙ SWIM Lesson:
Charitable Giving Can Reduce Taxes and Maximize Impact

Utilizing strategies like qualified charitable distributions (QCDs) and donor-advised funds (DAFs) can reduce your taxable income and leave a lasting legacy.

ACTION STEP: Identify a charity or cause that aligns with your values. Evaluate how tools like DAFs or QCDs can maximize your giving's impact while reducing your taxable estate.

> EXAMPLE
> - *Situation:* "I've been giving cash to my favorite charity each year, but I have appreciated stock in my portfolio."
> - *Action:* "I'll consult with my financial advisor about using a DAF to donate stock, avoid capital gains taxes, and maximize my deduction."

QUESTION: How can charitable giving strategies support causes you care about while reducing your tax liability? How might bunching these donations or utilizing appreciated stock impact your taxes?

_____

_____

_____

_____

_____

_____

CHAPTER EIGHT

Maximizing Two-Comma Wealth for Business Owners

The best way to predict the future is to create it.

—PETER DRUCKER

For many business owners, the word "exit" can feel unsettling. Your business is more than just a company—it's your passion, your life's work, and your legacy. But the reality is that 100 percent of business owners will eventually leave their companies, whether by choice or by circumstance. Forced exits where the business closes without selling are more common than many realize. This chapter is here to help you prepare for the inevitable by ensuring your business—likely your biggest asset—continues to fuel your two-comma wealth and secure your financial future. As Benjamin Franklin wisely said, "Failing to plan is planning to fail."

As a business owner who has achieved two-comma wealth, your company is likely the primary driver of your net worth. But just

As a business owner who has achieved two-comma wealth, your company is likely the primary driver of your net worth.

as you wouldn't rely on one vehicle for all your transportation needs (after all, it won't last forever, and you certainly can't drive it to Europe or the Bahamas), you shouldn't depend solely on one source to secure your financial future. By strategically planning for taxes, diversifying your investments, and crafting a well-thought-out exit strategy, you can protect and grow your wealth while securing your legacy.

In this chapter, we'll explore how you can do just that. As the president and a founder of the Orlando Chapter of the Exit Planning Institute (https://www.exit-planning-institute.org), I've helped numerous business owners assess their financial goals, create exit strategies, and implement business plans to protect their wealth. I encourage you to visit the Exit Planning Institute® website to find a local chapter near you and tap into the latest business owner exit strategies and network of professionals who specialize in these areas.

Let's dive into how you can maximize your two-comma wealth—starting with diversification, tax-saving strategies, and finally, planning your exit.

Diversifying Your Wealth: Don't Bet It All on Your Business

One of the most common mistakes I see business owners make is reinvesting everything back into their company. While that strategy might help grow your business, it can also leave your personal wealth vulnerable. Diversifying your wealth beyond your business is critical to ensuring your long-term financial security, no matter what challenges your business may face.

Here are two key ways to start building wealth outside your business:

Taxable Brokerage Accounts

A taxable brokerage account provides liquidity and flexibility, giving you the ability to invest in individual stocks, bonds, ETFs, and other assets. Unlike your business, these investments allow you to control when you trigger taxable events.

One of the most common mistakes I see business owners make is reinvesting everything back into their company.

I've worked with business owners who initially had nearly all their net worth tied up in their companies. By setting up taxable brokerage accounts and investing in tax-efficient ETFs and individual stocks, we created a diversified portfolio that provided financial stability, even during uncertain business periods. These accounts gave them more control over their financial future by reducing their reliance on their business for liquidity.

Maximizing Tax-Advantaged Retirement Plans

Retirement plans are one of the most effective tools for business owners to build personal wealth, save on taxes, and attract top talent. These plans offer not only tax-deferred growth but also significant tax incentives for the business itself. For those without an existing plan, establishing one may even provide additional tax credits for the setup costs, making it more affordable than you might think.

Over the past decade, I've worked with dozens of businesses to implement retirement plans of all types, helping them customize the right fit for their specific goals. Whether it's a Solo 401(k) for a sole proprietor or a cash balance plan for a larger enterprise, these plans can be tailored to provide substantial tax savings and long-term financial security.

Here are some options to consider:

401(k) Plans

For businesses of all sizes, 401(k) plans are a foundational option. They allow for both employee and employer contributions, offering a powerful tool for saving and retaining talent. For sole proprietors and their spouses, a Solo 401(k) provides similar benefits without the need for additional employees. Contributions made by the employer can also be excluded from payroll taxes, saving on both sides of the payroll tax.

- 2025 CONTRIBUTION LIMITS: $23,500 for employees under 50, with an extra $7,500 catch-up for those 50+ (or $11,250 for ages 60–63). Employers may contribute up to 25% of compensation, with an overall limit of $70,000—or more if catch-ups are utilized.
- ROTH OPTION: Many 401(k) plans now allow Roth contributions, providing tax-free growth and withdrawals in retirement. This flexibility benefits both the business owner and employees, empowering them to diversify their tax strategy. Note: Catch-up contributions for high earners must be made on a Roth basis beginning in 2026.

Profit-Sharing Plans

Profit-sharing plans allow businesses to reward employees based on company performance, creating alignment between employee efforts and the company's success. Contributions are flexible, allowing owners to adjust based on profitability.

- BENEFITS FOR OWNERS AND EMPLOYEES: These plans not only help retain top talent but also incentivize employees to think like business owners, especially when supported by regular education from a financial advisor.

Cash Balance Plans

Cash balance plans are a type of defined benefit plan ideal for high-income earners who want to accelerate retirement savings. Contributions can exceed $200,000 annually, depending on the participant's age, making them a great complement to a 401(k) or profit-sharing plan.

- KEY ADVANTAGE: Combining a cash balance plan with a 401(k) allows for six-figure contributions while minimizing tax liabilities.

SIMPLE IRA (Savings Incentive Match Plan for Employees Individual Retirement Account)

Designed for small businesses with one hundred or fewer employees, SIMPLE IRAs offer an easy-to-manage option with lower administrative costs.

- 2025 CONTRIBUTION LIMITS: $16,500 for employees under 50, plus a $3,500 catch-up for those over 50 (or $5,250 for ages 60–63). Employers must either match contributions (up to 3% of compensation) or provide a flat 2% contribution to all eligible employees.

SEP IRA (Simplified Employee Pension Individual Retirement Account)

SEP IRAs are another option for small business owners and self-employed individuals. Contributions are capped at 25 percent of compensation, up to $70,000 in 2025.

- FLEXIBILITY: Employers are not required to contribute every year, making it a good option for businesses with fluctuating income.

The Role of a Financial Advisor: Expertise You Can Trust

Selecting, implementing, and managing the right retirement plan for your business requires specialized knowledge. Over a decade ago, I earned the Chartered Retirement Plans Specialist℠ (CRPS®) designation, which has enabled me to help dozens of businesses set up and maintain retirement plans tailored to their unique needs. From Solo 401(k)s for sole proprietors to profit-sharing plans and cash balance plans for larger businesses, I've seen firsthand how these plans can create lasting value.

As a financial advisor with this specialized expertise, my role extends beyond just setting up the plan. I work with business owners to do the following:

- Identify the best retirement plan to fit their goals and structure, including options for Roth contributions.
- Educate employees on the benefits of the plan, fostering engagement and retention by showing that the company is invested in their future.
- Ensure compliance with ERISA regulations to reduce risks of legal or financial penalties, all while helping the business maximize tax savings.

Retirement plans are more than tax-advantaged savings vehicles—they're a tool to attract and retain top talent, align employee goals with company performance, and build long-term financial security for both the business owner and their team. My experience has shown that when retirement plans are designed strategically and supported by ongoing education, they not only save on taxes but also create a stronger, more motivated workforce.

Building a strong foundation for the future starts with proactive planning, and retirement plans are a crucial part of that equation. But as any seasoned business owner knows, life doesn't always follow the plan. While it's essential to focus on opportunities for growth, it's equally important to safeguard against the unexpected. That's where a defensive strategy becomes invaluable—not just for your business but for the two-comma wealth it supports.

The Five Ds: D-Fending Your Business Against Life's Unpredictable Events

As a business owner, you're likely focused on the future, always moving toward that next goal or new opportunity. But sometimes, the best offense is a good defense. Life has a way of throwing unexpected challenges at us, ones that even the most well-thought-out plans can't always anticipate. Mike Tyson famously said, "Everyone has a plan until they get punched in the face." For business owners, these "punches" can come from events we don't see coming: an unexpected health issue, a sudden family crisis, or a conflict with a key business partner.

The reality is we've all heard of these risks, but many business owners are convinced "it won't happen to me" or feel they simply don't have the time to address issues that seem so unlikely. But hope alone isn't a strategy, and when these events do strike, having a plan in place can make all the difference.

Sometimes, the best offense is a good defense.

That's why I'd like to share some real-world examples and statistics to bring these issues to the fore. These challenges are real, and the consequences of ignoring them can be substantial. The time you take now to prepare for these risks could be one of the best investments you make in your business. Known in exit planning as the "Five

Ds"—death, disability, divorce, disagreement, and distress—these challenges can derail even the best-laid plans if left unaddressed. Let's look at real-world examples of business owners who faced each of these scenarios and explore the practical D-Fense strategies that can safeguard your two-comma wealth and keep your business on solid ground.

1. Death: Ensuring Continuity Beyond Yourself

Did You Know?
According to the Exit Planning Institute's 2023 Owner Readiness Survey, 73 percent of privately held businesses expect to transition within the next decade, yet only 20 percent have a formal succession plan.[11] This leaves many businesses vulnerable if the owner suddenly passes away.

> EXAMPLE: Jim had spent twenty years building a successful landscaping business with loyal employees and clients. When he passed away unexpectedly, his wife, who was unfamiliar with the business, inherited his share. She faced tough decisions on managing or selling the company, while employees and clients worried about the company's future.

D-Fense Strategy

- SUCCESSION PLAN: Identify and train a successor to step in if you're no longer there, whether it's a trusted employee or family member.
- BUY-SELL AGREEMENT: This agreement allows for a smooth transfer of ownership to a business partner or key employee. In Jim's case, his wife could have sold her share to a

pre-determined partner, securing financial stability without operational responsibility.

- LIFE INSURANCE: Funding the buy-sell agreement with life insurance provides cash for buyouts, ensuring your family is financially protected without burdening them with managing the business.

By proactively planning for continuity, you protect the business you've built and ensure it continues fueling your two-comma wealth, even in your absence.

2. Disability: Securing Operational Resilience When You're Sidelined

Did You Know?
The Social Security Administration reports that one in four twenty-year-olds will become disabled before reaching retirement age.[12] Disability is one of the most common yet often-overlooked risks for business owners.

> EXAMPLE: Maria, the owner of a thriving digital marketing agency, suffered a severe back injury that left her unable to work for several months. Without Maria's leadership, her team struggled to manage projects effectively, and clients began to lose confidence in the agency's reliability. This drop in revenue threatened Maria's business and income.

D-Fense Strategy

- DISABILITY INSURANCE: Disability insurance replaces income during periods of incapacity, helping cover both personal and business expenses.

- DELEGATED AUTHORITY: Assigning power of attorney to a trusted employee or partner ensures critical decisions can still be made in your absence.
- DOCUMENTED PROCESSES: By documenting client workflows and key operations, Maria could have equipped her team to maintain services effectively, preventing client loss and preserving revenue.

Ensuring your business can continue without you safeguards your two-comma wealth from the unpredictable and preserves your income stream.

3. Divorce: Shielding Your Business from Personal Division

Did You Know?
The American Psychological Association estimates that 40–50 percent of marriages in the United States end in divorce, and when business assets are involved, these cases often become complex and financially draining.[13]

> EXAMPLE: Greg, co-owner of a growing tech startup, went through a sudden divorce. His spouse claimed a portion of his ownership as part of the settlement, putting Greg in a position where he faced losing control over the business or taking on a new partner he didn't choose.

D-Fense Strategy

- PRENUPTIAL/POSTNUPTIAL AGREEMENT: These agreements clarify asset ownership in case of a divorce, reducing potential legal disputes and protecting business interests.

- CLEAR FINANCIAL BOUNDARIES: Separate personal and business finances to make asset division simpler and to protect your company.
- BUY-SELL AGREEMENT WITH DIVORCE PROVISIONS: A buy-sell agreement with a divorce clause would allow Greg's business partner to buy out his ex-spouse's share, preserving the company's stability and structure.

By planning ahead for life's disruptions, you protect the business that fuels your two-comma wealth from personal challenges.

4. Disagreement: Preventing Internal Conflict from Derailing Your Business

Did You Know?

Research published in the Harvard Business Review reveals that 65 percent of high-potential startups fail due to conflicts among co-founders.[14] Managing disagreements effectively can be the difference between growth and failure.

> EXAMPLE: Amy and Sarah, cofounders of a fitness studio, initially agreed on every aspect of their business. But as it grew, they developed different visions—Amy wanted to open new locations, while Sarah prioritized online expansion. Their inability to reach a compromise created tension, leaving employees uncertain and slowing down decision-making, which affected growth and client satisfaction.

D-Fense Strategy

- OPERATING AGREEMENT: Define roles, responsibilities, and decision-making authority in an operating agreement to prevent power struggles and clarify roles.
- REGULAR COMMUNICATION: Structured meetings to discuss business goals can help partners stay aligned and address conflicts before they escalate.
- MEDIATION CLAUSE: Including a mediation clause in their partnership agreement allows partners to resolve disputes constructively, preserving both their relationship and the stability of the business.

Proactively preparing for disagreements protects the business that's driving your two-comma wealth from being sidetracked by conflict.

5. Distress: Building Financial Resilience Against Economic and Operational Shocks

Did You Know?
According to FEMA, 43 percent of businesses do not reopen after a large-scale disaster, and an additional 29 percent fail within two years of the disaster.[15] Financial resilience is essential to weathering unexpected challenges.

> EXAMPLE: During the COVID-19 pandemic, Paul's farm-to-table restaurant, known for its locally sourced ingredients and cozy dining experience, faced immense challenges. Lockdowns and social distancing measures led to a sharp decline in dine-in customers, and without a strong takeout or delivery setup, Paul saw his revenue plummet. Faced with high overhead costs and limited cash

flow, he was forced to close temporarily and lay off most of his staff, risking not only the future of his business but also his two-comma wealth.

D-Fense Strategy

- EMERGENCY FUND: Establishing a reserve fund to cover several months of essential expenses would have provided Paul with a financial buffer, allowing him to retain staff and keep the restaurant operating in a limited capacity during the crisis.
- REVENUE DIVERSIFICATION: If Paul had added alternative revenue sources—such as online cooking classes, meal kits, or a delivery menu—he could have continued engaging with customers and generating income, creating a more resilient business model less dependent on dine-in service.
- BUSINESS CONTINUITY PLAN: A continuity plan would have helped Paul quickly pivot to takeout and outdoor dining options, retaining a portion of his customer base and minimizing financial losses.

With a plan to weather unexpected distress, you create a business resilient enough to protect your two-comma wealth from sudden downturns.

These examples show that, while you can't predict every hit life might throw, you *can* prepare for it, and the peace of mind it can provide is priceless. Truth is, much like an insurance policy, I hope that investing in these strategies turns out to give you no financial return on investment at all—because that would mean none of these terrible events ever happen to you. But if they do, and the statistics clearly show they happen more often than we'd care to think, these D-Fensive strategies could prove to be the best investment of all.

With these foundational protections in place, you're ready to consider specific exit strategies that maximize the value of your business. Whether selling to an external buyer, transitioning to family, or implementing an employee buyout, a well-defended business will position you to achieve the best outcome for your two-comma wealth. Let's explore these options and the benefits each can bring to your future.

Planning Your Exit

No matter how successful your business is, planning your exit is crucial. Whether you want to sell, pass the business to family members, or implement an employee buyout, having an exit strategy ensures that you preserve the wealth you've built.

Regular business valuations are essential for understanding your company's worth and preparing for a successful exit. Whether your exit is planned or unexpected, knowing the value of your business allows you to negotiate confidently and ensure you're maximizing the returns on your life's work.

No matter how successful your business is, planning your exit is crucial.

When it comes to exit strategies for maximizing wealth, structuring your approach is crucial to reduce taxes and maximize what you take home. Let's walk through a few strategies to consider and their pros and cons.

1. **Stock Sale Versus Asset Sale**
    A stock sale is often more tax-efficient for sellers because it's typically taxed at lower long-term capital gains rates. However, buyers may be hesitant, as they inherit any company liabilities. On the other hand, an asset sale can be more appealing to buyers since they can depreciate the assets and avoid some liabilities. However,

the downside for you as the seller is that some assets may be taxed as ordinary income, which can lead to a higher tax bill.

2. **Employee Stock Ownership Plan (ESOP)**

    An ESOP can be a fantastic way to not only receive tax benefits but also ensure that your employees—those who know and care about the business—continue running it. Selling your business to employees through an ESOP allows for deferring capital gains taxes and can preserve your legacy. However, the process can be complex and costly to set up and maintain, and you may not receive the same sale price as you would from an outside buyer.

3. **Third-Party Sale**

    If maximizing the sale price is your primary goal, a third-party sale—whether to a strategic buyer or private equity firm—might be the way to go. This option often brings the highest sale price, especially if your business holds strategic value to the buyer. The downside is that you'll lose control over the company's future direction, and that may not align with your long-term vision for the business.

4. **Family Succession**

    A family succession plan can keep the business in the family and pass on your legacy. When structured with the right estate planning strategies, this option can be tax-efficient, but it may not bring in as much cash as a sale to an external buyer. Family dynamics can also complicate things, so clear planning and communication are essential here.

5. **Management Buyouts (MBO) and Mergers**

    An MBO allows your management team to buy you out, offering a smooth transition and continuity. However, depending on the team's financial resources, they may need outside financing, which can complicate the sale. A merger, on the other hand, can expand your company's market share but often presents challenges when integrating two companies, making it a more complex exit strategy.

But here's something to consider: If you find that you can't take a month-long vacation without your business falling apart, you might not have a business that's truly attractive to buyers. What you have is a job, not an investment. A Certified Exit Planning Advisor® (CEPA®) can help you implement new management techniques that not only reenergize you but also create a self-sustaining business that buyers will value more highly. In fact, this could even make you want to stay in the business longer!

Remember, this isn't an exhaustive list of exit strategies. Working with a CEPA®, tax advisors, and estate planners ensures that your strategy is fully tailored to your situation. They can also tap into their network to help find the right buyers, whether they're strategic investors, private equity firms, family, or management. The key is making sure your exit is structured in a way that maximizes both your wealth and your legacy while aligning with your long-term goals.

Is the Juice Worth the Squeeze?

One of the most challenging decisions any business owner—or in my father's case, a real estate investor—faces is knowing when it's time to let go of an asset. The question often boils down to: *Is the juice worth the squeeze?*

Take my dad, for example, and a recent heart-to-heart but eye-opening conversation we had not too long ago. Years ago, he purchased a house in need of major repairs for just $18,000. Over the years, he worked tirelessly to transform it, and he began renting it out for $800 a month. Today, that same property rents for $1,200 per month—a remarkable return on investment that he proudly points to as one of his best deals. The neighborhood has gentrified, driving up property values, and the house is now worth an impressive $350,000.

At first glance, this seems like a golden investment, and for years, it certainly was. But is it still? Let's break it down.

In a typical year, my father collects about $14,400 in rent. On the flip side, he pays $2,000 in property taxes and insurance (and we won't get into the fact he is underinsured on this property for the case of this illustration), spends about $1,000 on annual repairs, and generally

One of the most

challenging decisions any

business owner faces is

knowing when it's time

to let go of an asset.

faces a vacancy month each year, reducing his annual rent to $13,200. That leaves him with around $10,200 in income each year from the property. While this is an attractive figure, it becomes even more interesting when you consider what his return on investment (ROI) looks like today.

Given that the property is now worth $350,000, that $10,200 a year represents just under a 3 percent annual return. Setting aside investments in the stock market with varying levels of risk and potential for higher reward, if we assume in the current interest rate environment that he can get a 4.5 percent return on a "safe" investment like a certificate of deposit (CD) at the bank, how does that stack up? If he sold the property for $350,000 and placed the proceeds into such a CD, he could earn $15,750 annually—without any middle-of-the-night phone calls about broken toilets, without covering repair bills, without vacancy concerns or liability issues, and without the ongoing stress of being a landlord in general.

When you factor in the time, effort, and emotional energy required to maintain the property, you start to see that the "juice" he once squeezed out of this investment may no longer be worth it. That's a reality many business owners face when contemplating an exit. What was once a great deal—and still looks good on paper—might not be as valuable when compared to alternatives.

This isn't to say that keeping the property is the wrong choice. For some, the sense of control and the connection to the physical asset may outweigh the higher financial return of a more passive investment. There are, as we mentioned in chapter 5, taxes to consider, among other things. But as with any business, it's important to assess whether the value it provides in your eyes is worth the continued effort—or if it's time to pivot to something less physically and mentally taxing but equally, if not more, rewarding.

The question every business owner, investor, or landlord must ask themselves is this: *Is the juice still worth the squeeze?*

After carefully considering whether the juice is worth the squeeze—balancing the effort and rewards of selling your business—the next step is to determine whether the proceeds from the sale will truly meet your long-term financial needs. This is where understanding what the juice is worth and how that pairs with your wealth gap *becomes essential.*

Discovering Your Wealth Gap

One of the most important steps in aligning your personal financial goals with your business exit strategy is understanding your wealth gap—the difference between the assets you currently have and the amount you'll need to maintain your desired lifestyle after the sale of your business. This calculation helps you set a clear financial target and ensures your business exit strategy is built to close that gap.

To estimate your wealth gap, revisit the 4 percent rule discussed in chapter 2. This rule suggests that withdrawing 4 percent of your total portfolio annually allows for sustainable retirement income. Here's how you can apply it as a business owner:

1. Determine your desired *gross annual income in retirement (e.g., $200,000). This is your pretax income and should account for your living expenses, leisure activities, and unforeseen needs.*
2. Multiply that number by 25 to estimate the total portfolio size required (e.g., $200,000 × 25 = $5 million).
3. Subtract your current investable assets from this target to identify your wealth gap.
4. Ensure your *wealth gap accounts for the net proceeds from the sale of your business. Taxes and transaction costs can significantly reduce the proceeds, so it's critical to calculate the post-sale amount available to fill your gap.*

While this calculation provides a useful starting point, for a more precise number, it's essential to work with a financial advisor. This basic exercise gives you a ballpark on what you may need to cover your *needs*, but not necessarily your *wants* or *wishes*. And as we discussed in chapter 2, tools like Monte Carlo analysis can be used by your financial advisor to simulate thousands of potential market scenarios, providing a more accurate projection of how your portfolio might perform under various conditions. These advanced tools ensure you're relying on reliable data when planning your exit and determining how much your business sale needs to contribute to meet your goals.

Example

Let's say you currently have $2 million in investments but need $5 million to retire comfortably. Your wealth gap is $3 million. However, if the sale of your business is expected to generate $3 million, you'll need to calculate the net proceeds after taxes and fees. For instance, if 25 percent of the sale is lost to taxes and transaction costs, your net proceeds will only be $2.25 million—leaving a $750,000 short-fall. Understanding this early allows you to plan for strategies that reduce taxes, such as installment sales, deferred compensation, or trust structures.

Identifying your wealth gap is not just about numbers—it's about creating a foundation for financial security and independence. By accounting for taxes, transaction costs, and other potential reductions, you can take steps to maximize your business's value, negotiate effectively, and ensure your personal financial goals are met. This insight is the cornerstone of a well-planned business exit and the bridge between where you are now and the future you envision.

With your wealth gap calculated and your business strategy aligned to meet your financial needs, you're ready to start thinking about what comes next. Beyond the numbers lies a new chapter of purpose, fulfillment, and impact—let's explore what's waiting for you beyond the exit.

Beyond the Exit

Exiting your business isn't just about dollars and cents—it's about legacy. Whether you're selling to a third party, passing the business to family, or implementing an employee buyout, your exit will have a lasting impact on the company and the people who depend on it. By thoughtfully planning your exit, you can ensure that your business continues to thrive and that the legacy you've built endures long after you step away.

One of our clients, deeply invested in the future of her community, worked with me to put together a family transition plan that ensured the business would continue serving the community for generations to come. It wasn't just about financial success—it was about ensuring her values and impact lived on.

Next Steps: Securing Your Wealth and Purpose

Throughout this book, we've discussed strategies for growing and protecting your wealth. In chapter 7, we explored how estate planning can safeguard your legacy. Now, as we approach chapter 9, we'll focus on the final piece of the puzzle—purpose-driven planning.

We'll discuss practical steps to avoid scams, secure your wealth from modern threats, and ensure your financial success continues to support the meaningful life you've built. Let's make sure that all your hard work not only leads to financial security but also enables you to live with purpose and protect the legacy you've created.

SWIM Lesson 8

SWIM Lesson:
Diversify Beyond Your Business

Relying solely on your business for wealth is risky. Diversifying investments ensures long-term financial stability and reduces dependency on a single income source.

ACTION STEP: Review your net worth statement and identify what percentage of your assets are tied to your business. Take one small step today to diversify, such as earmarking a portion of your next business profits for an investment account or researching options to gradually reallocate assets into other investments.

EXAMPLE
- *Situation:* "My net worth statement shows 80 percent of my wealth is tied to my business."
- *Action:* "I'll allocate 10 percent of this year's business profits to a diversified portfolio and consult my advisor about rebalancing my overall asset allocation."

QUESTION: Have you diversified your personal wealth outside of your business? What steps can you take now to build a more balanced financial portfolio?

_____

_____

_____

_____

⊕ SWIM Lesson:
Maximize Tax-Advantaged Retirement Plans

Using tax-efficient retirement accounts helps grow wealth, reduce taxes, and retain key employees.

ACTION STEP: Evaluate your retirement plan options—Solo 401(k)s, SEP IRAs, and Cash Balance Plans—to determine the best fit for your business and personal financial goals.

> EXAMPLE
> - *Situation:* "I want to lower my taxable income while creating retirement savings for my team."
> - *Action:* "I'll consult with a financial advisor to establish a cash balance plan for my business, ensuring it aligns with my long-term financial goals."

QUESTION: Are you maximizing retirement plans to save for the future while reducing taxes? How could offering competitive plans improve employee retention?

_____

_____

_____

_____

_____

_____

_____

_____

_____

⊕ SWIM Lesson:
Plan for Life's Unexpected Events

Establishing strategies to counter the five Ds—death, disability, divorce, disagreement, and distress—protects your business and wealth.

ACTION STEP: Develop a contingency plan to address risks like illness, disputes, or other disruptions. Ensure you have agreements, insurance, and a business continuity plan in place.

> EXAMPLE
> - *Situation:* "I worry about how my business would continue if I were suddenly incapacitated."
> - *Action:* "I'll work with my legal and financial advisors to establish a buy-sell agreement and disability insurance to safeguard the company."

QUESTION: Have you considered the greatest risks your business might face? How prepared are you for events like illness, unexpected conflicts, or economic downturns?

_____

_____

_____

_____

_____

_____

_____

_____

⊙ SWIM Lesson:
Create a Comprehensive Exit Strategy

Planning your business exit early allows you to maximize its value and secure your financial future.

ACTION STEP: Conduct regular business valuations and explore exit options like ESOPs, third-party sales, or family succession to determine what best fits your goals.

> EXAMPLE
> - *Situation:* "I want to retire in five years but don't know what my business is worth or how to transition out."
> - *Action:* "I'll schedule a valuation this year and begin discussions with a Certified Exit Planning Advisor® to outline my exit options."

QUESTION: What does your ideal business exit look like? Are you actively working on an exit strategy that aligns with your financial and personal objectives?

_____

_____

_____

_____

_____

_____

_____

_____

_____

_____

⊕ SWIM Lesson:
Consider the Tax Implications of Your Exit

The structure of your exit—whether a stock sale, asset sale, or ESOP—has significant tax implications that impact the wealth you take home.

ACTION STEP: Meet with a tax advisor to evaluate how different exit strategies will impact your financial outcome. Identify ways to optimize taxes and preserve wealth.

> EXAMPLE
> - *Situation:* "I'm considering selling my business but don't know how much I'll actually keep after taxes."
> - *Action:* "I'll meet with a tax advisor to explore whether a stock sale or installment sale would minimize my tax liability and increase my net proceeds."

QUESTION: Have you consulted with experts to ensure your exit strategy is tax-efficient? How might structuring your exit differently maximize your wealth?

_____

_____

_____

_____

_____

_____

_____

_____

_____

CHAPTER NINE

Purpose-Driven Planning

The real measure of your wealth is how much
you'd be worth if you lost all your money.

—UNKNOWN

Your hard work, intuition, and dedication have brought you to this point, and your decision to read this book is a testament to your desire to be a good steward of your wealth. Now, it's time to move forward with purpose, ensuring that money is not just a number but a tool to enhance your life, create lasting memories, and secure your legacy for future generations.

Memory Dividends

Bill Perkins, author of *Die with Zero,* offers the concept of "memory dividends," which highlights the value of using money to create meaningful experiences that continue to pay emotional and psychological dividends over time.[16] Financial wealth is important, but so is the wealth that comes from a lifetime of cherished memories.

Financial wealth is

important, but so is

the wealth that comes

from a lifetime of

cherished memories.

Think back to your own life—what are the moments that stand out? It's likely the trips you've taken with loved ones, the milestones you've celebrated, or even the simpler moments of joy. These experiences are what make life rich, not just the balance in your investment accounts. The key is balancing financial prudence with creating a life full of memories that you can look back on with satisfaction.

Over the decades, life evolves in five-to-ten-year windows, with changes that we can't always predict. What brings you joy today may shift over time. For instance, I used to be a roller coaster enthusiast in my younger years, but now, with two teenage daughters, the thrill has faded, and I often find myself needing a lot more convincing to get on those rides. Still, I get to experience that excitement vicariously through my daughters and look back fondly on the days when I was bold enough to embrace every twist and turn—when my back could handle the jolts, and my fear of heights was a little more subdued. This really illustrates how both our tolerance for risk and life's circumstances are always shifting and how the opportunities to create meaningful memories evolve along with them.

The Power of Rebalancing and Recalibrating

We often think of rebalancing only in terms of our financial portfolios, but rebalancing applies to our lives and priorities too—I call that recalibrating. Just as your investment portfolio requires periodic adjustments to stay aligned with your long-term goals, your approach to life, experiences, and spending should also be recalibrated.

Your portfolio might grow scattered over time—assets in multiple accounts, investments in various funds—and if left unchecked, it can become unwieldy. The same is true for your focus in life. It's easy to accumulate more things instead of investing in meaningful experiences. That's why it's essential to step back, assess your goals, and ensure that your assets—both financial and emotional—are working together to enrich your life.

For example, we discussed the importance of estate planning in chapter 7. When my wife Kristin and I went on our first short trip without the kids, we revisited our estate plan, particularly our will and the choice of guardians for our children. At the time, we agreed that Kristin's best friend from childhood, who lived on the West Coast, would be the guardian for our then-toddler daughters, even though we live on the East Coast. Fast forward a decade, and our children are now settled with their friends and routines. In the unfortunate event that something happened to both of us, moving 2,400 miles away would be incredibly disruptive to their lives. Times and circumstances change, and so do our goals. That's why it's so important to recalibrate our plans to reflect these changes.

Every six months or so, revisit both your portfolio and your personal goals. Are your investments supporting your life, or are they just numbers on a statement? Are you aligning your resources with your priorities—whether that means funding experiences, securing your future, or supporting causes you care about? Regular rebalancing keeps everything on track, whether you're managing money or curating a life filled with meaning.

Your portfolio might grow scattered over time—assets in multiple accounts, investments in various funds—and if left unchecked, it can become unwieldy.

Focus on What You Can Control

As your wealth grows, so too does the feeling that the stakes are higher—market swings seem larger, tax changes feel more impactful, and the unpredictability of it all can be unsettling. For those who've built their two-comma wealth by staying in control—making strategic decisions and planning carefully—facing the reality that some things are simply out of your hands can be overwhelming.

But here's the truth: While you can't control everything, there's still plenty you can do. And often, narrowing your focus to the things you can control not only brings clarity but keeps you from falling into the trap of reacting to every headline or market move.

Think about the markets for a moment. You can't predict or influence how they'll perform day-to-day, especially as they're driven by countless factors far beyond your reach. However, you can control how you structure your portfolio. You can make sure it's diversified, set to weather volatility, and aligned with your long-term goals. Trying to outsmart the market on a regular basis is a recipe for anxiety, but focusing on a sound strategy allows you to ride out the inevitable ups and downs, preserving the wealth you've worked so hard to build.

The same goes for taxes and estate planning. While tax laws and estate regulations are constantly evolving, and those changes may feel like a moving target, what you can control is how prepared you are for those shifts. Working closely with professionals who stay on top of these developments ensures your strategy stays optimized, protecting your wealth from unnecessary erosion. You don't need to predict every change; you just need a plan that adapts as the rules do.

This principle is especially important if you're a business owner planning your exit. You can't control the broader economy or guarantee the perfect buyer will arrive when you're ready to sell. But you can control how prepared your business is for a sale—keeping your finances in order and positioning the company to attract the right offers. These are actionable steps within your control that set you up for a smoother, more successful transition.

At this stage, managing two-comma wealth isn't just about growing it further—it's about ensuring it works efficiently for you and your family. The challenge lies in not getting distracted by every external force, especially when the numbers involved can make those forces feel scarier. But the media's job is to stir fear, focusing on uncontrollable events that keep you tuned in. The truth is that reacting to every piece of bad news or every economic change is exhausting and, more importantly, counterproductive. By honing in on what's within your control—your investment strategy, tax efficiency, estate plans, and business readiness—you ensure your wealth continues to serve you without letting the outside noise throw you off course.

Of course, you don't have to do it all alone. A good advisor can act as your coach, helping you filter out the distractions and keep your focus on what truly matters. By working together, they can help you stay grounded, ensuring your wealth management aligns with your goals and continues to support your purpose, rather than being swayed by things that don't move the needle.

Taxes, Estate Laws, and Staying Vigilant

A crucial aspect of maintaining and growing your wealth is recognizing that taxes, estate laws, and financial regulations are constantly evolving. What works today may not be the best strategy tomorrow. This is why staying vigilant and working closely with trusted advisors who stay up to date on these changes is essential.

Your financial advisor should be someone who actively monitors the tax code and estate law adjustments, ensuring your wealth remains optimized, and they should work closely with you and your tax professional. Small oversights in tax strategy or estate planning can have significant financial consequences. Tax laws or estate tax thresholds can change, and if you aren't prepared, a large portion of your wealth could be eroded by avoidable taxes.

Likewise, when choosing a tax professional, don't just settle for someone who files your return and calls it a day. You want a forward-thinking tax planner, someone who can forecast scenarios for next year and work with your financial advisor to build a strategy. The focus should be on long-term planning, not just this year's refund. Avoid "cutting your nose to spite your face." A great tax pro won't just look backward for deductions—they'll help chart a proactive course for minimizing your tax burden over the years. It may take some interviewing, but they're out there.

By staying ahead of these changes and working with professionals who understand how to adapt your strategy accordingly, you can ensure your estate plan is efficient and aligned with your long-term goals. This vigilance is key to preserving your wealth and passing it smoothly to the next generation, minimizing the risk of sudden financial surprises.

The Annuity Safety Trap and "Magic Math"

Annuities are often marketed as a secure retirement solution, promising guaranteed income for life. On the surface, they appear to be the perfect safety net—offering peace of mind in a volatile market. However, these products often come with high fees, limited flexibility, and what I call "magic math."

This magic math refers to the way annuity illustrations are presented to make the product seem more lucrative than it is. For example, they might emphasize "guaranteed growth" or "lifetime payouts" without fully disclosing the fees, surrender charges, or the opportunity cost of locking up your money in a low-growth product.

Dr. Moshe Milevsky, a leading expert on retirement income, aptly points out in *The 7 Most Important Equations for Your Retirement*:[17] "Annuities are not a panacea; they are tools, and like all tools, their value depends on how and when they are used." While annuities can serve a specific purpose, their complexity and cost structures often outweigh the benefits for many retirees.

The truth is, annuities are just one example of many complex financial products that can be overwhelming to navigate. Whether it's certain types of permanent life insurance policies, structured notes, or alternative investments, the appeal of "customized solutions" often hides significant trade-offs. High fees, illiquidity, and lack of transparency are issues that are not exclusive to annuities but can be present in a wide range of financial products.

Annuities can be a lot like magic shows—impressive on the surface, but the trick is in what they don't show you.

Let me be clear: Complexity doesn't necessarily mean a product is bad. Financial products like annuities, life insurance, or structured investments can have a place in a well-rounded portfolio, depending on the goals and needs of the investor. However, their value comes down to how well they are understood and whether they align with your overall financial plan. A product that may be appropriate for one person can be an unnecessary expense for another.

Here's where the golden rule of investing comes in: *If you don't fully understand it, don't buy it.* To avoid the trap of "magic math," always seek a second opinion from a trusted advisor. A fiduciary advisor, who is obligated to act in your best interest, can help you navigate these decisions and ensure that your money is working for you in a way that aligns with your goals.

Annuities can be a lot like magic shows—impressive on the surface, but the trick is in what they don't show you.

For those seeking investment income, there are often better strategies, such as creating your own income stream using a combination of dividend-paying stocks, bonds, or even a systematic withdrawal strategy. These approaches provide greater flexibility and can often deliver comparable results without the downsides of certain contracts.

By understanding the true costs and trade-offs—not just with annuities but with any complex financial product—you can ensure your wealth is not only preserved but also working efficiently for you. An informed decision is always the best decision.

Financial Fraud: How to Protect Yourself

As your wealth grows,

so does the risk of being

targeted by increasingly

sophisticated schemes.

Over the years, I've sadly seen many fall victim to various scams that target individuals with two-comma wealth. As your wealth grows, so does the risk of being targeted by increasingly sophisticated schemes. Let's talk through some of the recent ones I've encountered and, more importantly, how you can protect yourself.

1. The "Child-in-Distress" Scam

One of the most emotionally charged scams out there is the "child-in-distress" con. Imagine getting a call that sounds exactly like your child, claiming they've been arrested abroad and need money fast. With AI technology, these fraudsters can mimic voices to make the situation feel scarily real.

HOW TO PROTECT YOURSELF: Always take a step back. Verify the story by contacting your child or another family member directly. Scammers use urgency to get you to act quickly, so slowing down is often the first line of defense.

2. The IRS Debt Collection Scam

Several clients have received terrifying calls supposedly from the IRS, threatening legal action or jail time if immediate payment isn't made. They'll demand payment via wire transfers or even gift cards, which should be a major red flag.

HERE'S THE TRUTH: The IRS never contacts you this way. They communicate through official letters. If you receive such a call, hang up and verify the legitimacy with your tax professional or the IRS directly.

3. Slip-and-Fall or Car Accident Fraud

I've also seen cases where clients have been the target of staged accidents—whether it's a "slip and fall" on their property or a car accident designed to lead to a lawsuit. These fraudsters hope to extract large settlements, banking on the fact that you have significant wealth.

YOUR PROTECTION: This is where, as discussed in chapter 7, having suitable property and casualty insurance and an umbrella policy is critical. These policies provide that extra safety net, ensuring you're not vulnerable to opportunistic lawsuits.

The Role of a Trusted Financial Advisor

One of the best ways to shield yourself from fraud—and poor financial decisions—is by working closely with a fiduciary financial advisor. I've helped many clients navigate these challenges, not just by managing their investments but by acting as a partner in their financial lives. A fiduciary advisor is legally obligated to act in your best interest and is someone who helps you with everything from managing risk to planning your legacy. When hiring a financial advisor, look for someone with the CERTIFIED FINANCIAL PLANNER™ (CFP®) designation, as a CERTIFIED FINANCIAL PLANNER™ professional is held to a fiduciary standard and brings an additional level of expertise beyond just their investment advice. A trusted advisor can do the following:

- FACILITATE FAMILY MEETINGS to ensure clear communication about estate plans and goals.
- COORDINATE WITH YOUR PROFESSIONAL TEAM—your accountant, estate lawyer, and other advisors—to make sure your financial strategy is cohesive and optimized.
- BE UP FRONT AND HONEST, even when it's difficult. A great advisor will push you to stay aspirational but keep you grounded and help you avoid otherwise costly mistakes.
- ENCOURAGE PROACTIVE ACTION, from reviewing estate plans to staying updated on tax strategies, making sure you're always one step ahead.

An additional safeguard is designating a *trusted contact* on your accounts. This person is someone your advisor can reach out to if they notice suspicious activity or concerning signs, such as unusual spending or cognitive decline. Having someone like this in place offers peace of mind, knowing your wealth is protected even if you're unable to manage things yourself.

These scams are real and, unfortunately, more common than you'd think. But with the right protections and a trusted advisor by your side, you can stay ahead of the risks and focus on enjoying the life you've worked so hard to build.

What to Look for in a Financial Advisor

Choosing the right financial advisor is one of the most important decisions you'll make. Managing two-comma wealth requires more than just basic financial advice—it takes specialized knowledge, a comprehensive approach, and someone who understands the complexities of high-net-worth individuals. A proactive advisor will anticipate challenges and opportunities before they arise, ensuring your financial strategy adapts as your needs evolve rather than reacting after issues occur.

First, consider looking for an advisor with at least ten years of experience. There's something to be said for "gray-headedness"—it's often a crown of beauty, a sign of wisdom gained through years of navigating both market highs and lows. But experience alone isn't enough. You want an advisor who still has plenty of runway ahead, someone who won't be retiring around the same time as you. The last thing you want is to be passed down to a junior associate because your advisor is retiring with or before you. Finding an advisor who is experienced yet also committed to being there for you in the long term is key to ensuring continuity in your financial plan.

Managing two-comma wealth requires more than just basic financial advice—it takes specialized knowledge, a comprehensive approach, and someone who understands the complexities of high-net-worth individuals.

In addition to experience and longevity, look for an advisor with a dedicated team. Solo advisors, while well-meaning, may not have the bandwidth to provide the level of service that high-net-worth individuals require. A strong internal team allows your advisor to deliver timely service, offer proactive communication, and ensure your financial needs are met without being stretched too thin. If anything were to happen to your primary advisor, having a team in place ensures that your financial plan continues smoothly, providing you with peace of mind.

Beyond technical skills and qualifications, it's essential to find an advisor with high emotional intelligence (EQ), not just intellectual intelligence (IQ). Managing wealth is about more than numbers—it's about understanding what matters most to you personally. You want an advisor who takes the time to ask meaningful questions, listens carefully to your goals, and helps you explore how your financial decisions can align with the highest levels of Maslow's hierarchy of needs, like self-actualization and fulfillment. This requires someone who can guide you in using your wealth to create a life of purpose and meaning, not just grow your portfolio.

An advisor with strong EQ will help you navigate the topics covered in this book that matter to you—whether it's achieving financial security, creating lasting memories, or establishing a legacy for future generations. They should be a trusted partner who helps you reflect on what brings you joy and how to use your financial success to enhance your life.

Two-comma wealth individuals often need specialized services in areas like estate planning and tax strategy. A knowledgeable and well-connected advisor can tap into this network when needed, ensuring you receive the best guidance from experts in those fields.

For those with significant wealth—typically $5 million or more in investable assets—working with a Certified Private Wealth Advisor® (CPWA®) professional is especially important. I completed my CPWA® coursework through Yale University and can personally attest to the scholarship and rigor this designation entails. This rigorous training equips advisors with deep knowledge of investment, tax, and estate strategies specifically designed for individuals well into their two-comma wealth.

Two-comma wealth individuals often need specialized services in areas like estate planning and tax strategy.

For clients, this means confidence in working with an advisor who understands the unique challenges and opportunities that come with significant wealth, as well as the strategies needed to address them effectively. A CPWA® professional specializes in addressing the unique challenges of high-net-worth individuals, providing advanced strategies like wealth transfer, legacy planning, and sophisticated tax optimization. Their training focuses on making sure your wealth continues to grow and is passed on efficiently.

For business owners, it's wise to seek out a CEPA® professional and likely a team of such professionals across financial, legal, and accounting industries to start. A CEPA® professional can help you develop a strategy to maximize the value of your business and plan a smooth exit that aligns with your financial and personal goals. Similarly, if you provide retirement plans for your employees, working with a Chartered Retirement Plans Specialist℠ (CRPS®) professional can help you design tax-efficient retirement plans that not only benefit your employees but also help you retain top talent.

In my own career, I've not just pursued but achieved each of these designations—Certified Financial Planner™ (CFP®), Certified Private Wealth Advisor® (CPWA®), Certified Exit Planning Advisor® (CEPA®), and Chartered Retirement Plans Specialist℠ (CRPS®)—because I am committed to being a lifelong learner. Despite being a Forbes-recognized top advisor at my firm, I haven't rested on my experience alone, and neither should your advisor. Instead, I've earned these designations to ensure I can provide my clients with the most up-to-date strategies, tools, and insights available, no matter how complex their financial needs are. This commitment to continuous learning is something you should seek in your own advisor—someone who isn't just relying on past success but constantly striving to offer the best solutions for your financial future.

Ultimately, the right advisor is more than just someone who manages your investments.

Ultimately, the right advisor is more than just someone who manages your investments. They should act as a guide through life's changes, help facilitate important family discussions, and work alongside your team of other professionals—like your accountant, estate attorney, and tax advisor. A great advisor will challenge you to think big but also ensure that your financial strategies are practical and aligned with your long-term goals.

When you find an advisor who has the experience, emotional intelligence, credentials, and team to support you, you're ensuring that your wealth is not just growing but being protected and aligned with the life you want to live. At two-comma wealth, your financial needs go beyond what an average advisor can offer—you need someone with specialized expertise, the ability to navigate complex tax and estate strategies, and a deeper understanding of how to align your wealth with your long-term goals and values. Make sure you choose someone who will be there for you—not just today, but for the long haul.

Money as a Tool for Meaningful Living

The underlying theme of this book is that money is a tool—a tool to create a meaningful life, not an end in itself. By now, you've reached a point in your life where you've accumulated significant wealth. But the true value of that wealth lies in how you use it. It's not just about investing wisely or avoiding the traps of financial gimmicks; it's about aligning your money with your values and purpose.

The underlying theme of this book is that money is a tool—a tool to create a meaningful life, not an end in itself.

Take time to think deeply about what matters most to you. Is it spending time with loved ones? Is it traveling the world, building memories with your family, or supporting causes you believe in? Use your financial resources to create a life filled with these experiences. Money is the fuel that can help drive your life forward, but it's the experiences, relationships, and impact you leave behind that will ultimately matter most.

Remember: Being a good steward of your wealth means using it to live fully—not just accumulating it for the sake of having more. With the right balance of financial discipline, purposeful spending, and a focus on meaningful living, you can enjoy the rewards of both financial freedom and a rich, fulfilling life.

Remember: Being a good steward of your wealth means using it to live fully—not just accumulating it for the sake of having more.

SWIM Lesson 9

SWIM Lesson:
Money as a Tool for Meaningful Living

Use your wealth to create meaningful experiences that pay emotional and psychological dividends over time.

ACTION STEP: Identify one personal or faith-based value that deeply resonates with you (e.g., supporting your local congregation, funding educational opportunities for underserved communities, or fostering family unity). Take one small step today to align your wealth with that value, such as starting a recurring donation, planning a faith-based family project, or exploring charitable giving strategies.

> EXAMPLE
> - *Situation:* "I want to strengthen my faith community while fostering family involvement."
> - *Action:* "I'll organize a family donation to help fund a community service project through my place of worship and set a goal to volunteer together."

QUESTION: How have your recent experiences brought you joy, and what opportunities do you see to create even more meaningful moments?

_____

_____

_____

_____

⊕ SWIM Lesson:
Rebalance and Recalibrate Regularly

Just as financial portfolios need rebalancing, your life goals and spending priorities should be recalibrated over time to reflect evolving values.

ACTION STEP: Schedule a review of your personal and financial goals at least twice a year to ensure they align with your current values and future aspirations.

EXAMPLE
- *Situation:* "I realized our family priorities shifted now that our kids are teenagers."
- *Action:* "I'll review our family budget and consider redirecting resources toward shared experiences like travel rather than individual activities."

QUESTION: What has changed in your life recently that might require you to adjust your financial goals or priorities?

_____

_____

_____

_____

_____

_____

_____

_____

_____

ACT

SWIM Lesson:
Stay Vigilant with Taxes and Estate Planning

Tax laws and estate planning regulations evolve, and staying proactive with your strategies ensures your wealth is protected and passed on smoothly.

ACTION STEP: Review your tax and estate plans with trusted professionals to confirm they're optimized and compliant with current laws.

> EXAMPLE
> - *Situation:* "I heard about upcoming changes in estate tax thresholds."
> - *Action:* "I'll schedule a meeting with my financial advisor and estate attorney to ensure my current plan aligns with the new regulations."

QUESTION: What steps can you take now to ensure your tax and estate plans remain aligned with your evolving goals and the latest regulations?

_____

_____

_____

_____

_____

_____

_____

_____

⊕ SWIM Lesson:
Avoid the "Magic Math" Trap

Be cautious of financial products that seem too good to be true, like high-fee annuities or complex investments.

ACTION STEP: Evaluate the financial products in your portfolio. Seek a second opinion from a fiduciary advisor for any strategies you don't fully understand.

> EXAMPLE
> - *Situation:* "I was offered an investment with 'guaranteed' returns that seemed high compared to my portfolio."
> - *Action:* "I'll consult my fiduciary advisor to review the product and compare its features to more transparent alternatives."

QUESTION: What questions do you have about your current financial products, and how can you ensure they truly support your goals?

_____

_____

_____

_____

_____

_____

_____

_____

_____

◈ SWIM Lesson:
Find an Advisor with Both IQ and EQ

Managing two-comma wealth requires more than just technical knowledge. Look for an advisor with high emotional intelligence (EQ) who takes the time to understand your values, goals, and what brings meaning to your life.

ACTION STEP: Share some of the strategies in this book and the goals you've set through the SWIM Lessons with your advisor. Gauge their familiarity with these topics and evaluate whether they and their team have the ability to meet your expectations after reading this book.

> EXAMPLE
> - *Situation:* "I want my advisor to understand the strategies I've learned and provide proactive insights into implementing them."
> - *Action:* "I'll schedule a meeting to discuss my goals and evaluate their ability to help me achieve them, particularly in areas like tax planning, legacy building, and meaningful living."

QUESTION: Does your advisor demonstrate both technical expertise (IQ) and emotional understanding (EQ)? Are they and their team equipped to support your goals as outlined in this book?

_____

_____

_____

_____

_____

CONCLUSION

L ooking at life through my father's eyes has profoundly shaped the way I approach wealth and financial advising. He achieved two-comma wealth through a lifetime of hard work. His dream when he immigrated to America was simple: to save enough money to build a home in Katerini, Greece. Some fifty years later, through perseverance, savings, and careful planning, he fulfilled that dream—a testament to what dedication and a clear goal can accomplish.

As I helped my father sort through his financial "junk drawer," I came to realize his definition of wealth was far more expansive than a bank account balance. His true wealth lies in the memories he's created, the family he's nurtured, and the experiences he's cherished. Money was simply the tool that allowed him to live his values and build a legacy that transcends dollars.

My father's journey reminds us all that wealth is not just about financial success—it's about using that success to live a life of purpose, fulfillment, and joy. You've worked hard to build your own wealth, but its true value lies in how you use it: to create lasting memories, provide for loved ones, and support the causes that matter most to you.

The journey of wealth isn't just about accumulation; it's about intention. Now that you've reached a level of financial success, the next step is to balance the security your wealth provides with the opportunities it offers to live fully and meaningfully.

Life will always be unpredictable—market fluctuations, unexpected expenses, and personal changes are inevitable. But as we've explored throughout this book, staying proactive and adaptive ensures that these twists and turns don't derail your goals. It's how you navigate life's challenges that defines your long-term success.

One constant in life is change, particularly in areas like taxes, estate laws, financial strategies, and investment tools. Staying informed and working closely with a trusted team of advisors ensures that your financial strategy evolves with the times and remains optimized to protect your two-comma wealth. By the time you're reading this, some laws and strategies may have already shifted—some subtly, others significantly. That's the nature of finance: It doesn't stand still. A book, by design, can't update in real time, but the core principles and approaches shared here will always be relevant. And while this book covers many of the most impactful ways to build and protect wealth, no single resource can address every unique situation. That's why working with a trusted financial advisor, accountant, and attorney isn't just important—it's essential.

Throughout this book, I've shared the importance of having a great financial advisor, and for good reason. A fiduciary advisor doesn't just manage your money; they help you plan for your future, facilitate meaningful family discussions, and align your wealth with your long-term vision. They'll stay ahead of changes in tax and estate laws, evolving investment strategies, and advancements in financial planning tools—ensuring your strategy remains up to date and aligned with your goals. More importantly, a great financial advisor serves as the central point of coordination, working alongside your accountant, attorney, and other professionals to ensure every aspect of your financial life is aligned and optimized.

CONCLUSION

As much as I've packed this book with actionable insights, true financial success requires more than just reading—it requires action. I encourage you to go back and review your answers to the Stefanou Wealth and Investment Management (SWIM) Lessons included throughout this book. These lessons are designed to help you align your wealth with your values and take actionable steps toward a fulfilling life. Revisiting your answers periodically can help ensure you stay on track as your circumstances and goals evolve. Take what you've learned here, share it with your advisor, and begin putting it into practice. And if this book has helped you, I encourage you to pass it on to someone else who might benefit from its lessons.

If you'd like to purchase additional copies for friends and family or simply keep up with where this book gets featured as time goes on, you can visit www.twocommawealth.com. Sharing knowledge is one of the best ways to inspire others on their own journeys toward financial stewardship and fulfillment.

I hope this book has given you valuable insights into aligning your wealth with your goals and values. My wish is that it inspires you to take meaningful steps toward a life of purpose and financial security. Thank you for allowing me to be part of your journey. Perhaps our paths will cross someday, and I would be honored to hear about the impact this book has had on your life.

ENDNOTES

1 James Grubman and Dennis T. Jaffe, "Immigrants and Natives to Wealth: Understanding Clients Based on Their Wealth Origins," *Journal of Financial Planning* 20, no. 7 (July 2007): 26–33.

2 John Jennings, "Money Buys Happiness After All," *Forbes*, February 12, 2024, https://www.forbes.com/sites/johnjennings/2024/02/12/money-buys-happiness-after-all/?sh=79440518486b.

3 Daniel Kahneman and Angus Deaton, "High Income Improves Evaluation of Life but Not Emotional Well-Being," *Proceedings of the National Academy of Sciences*, 107, no. 38 (2010), 16489–16493, https://doi.org/10.1073/pnas.1011492107.

4 Ric Edelman, "You're Making Big Financial Mistakes—and It's Your Brain's Fault," CNBC, July 31, 2019, https://www.cnbc.com/2019/07/31/youre-making-big-financial-mistakes-and-its-your-brains-fault.html.

5 "Quantitative Analysis of Investor Behavior," DALBAR, Inc., 2023, https://www.dalbar.com/ProductsAndServices/QAIB

6 Francis M. Kinniry Jr., et al., "Putting a Value on Your Value: Quantifying Vanguard Advisor's Alpha®," Vanguard Research, August 12, 2022, https://advisors.vanguard.com/insights/article/putting-a-value-on-your-value-quantifying-advisors-alpha.

7 Paul G. Firth, Hui Zheng, Jeremy S. Windsor, Andrew I. Sutherland, Christopher H. Imray, G. W. K. Moore, John L. Semple, Robert C. Roach, Richard A Salisbury, "Mortality on Mount Everest, 1921–2006: Descriptive Study," The BMJ 337:a2654 (2008), https://www.bmj.com/content/337/bmj.a2654.

8   Philip L. Cooley, Carl M. Hubbard, and Daniel T. Walz, "Retirement Savings: Choosing a Withdrawal Rate That Is Sustainable," *The American Association of Individual Investors Journal* 20, no. 2 (1998): 16–21.

9   Daniel Kahneman and Angus Deaton, "High Income Improves Evaluation of Life but Not Emotional Well-Being," *Proceedings of the National Academy of Sciences* 107, no. 38 (2010): 16489–16493.

10   David Bach, "The Latte Factor: Why You Don't Have to Be Rich to Live Rich" (Atria Books, 2019).

11   2023 National State of Owner Readiness Report, Exit Planning Institute, https://exit-planning-institute.org/2023-national-state-of-owner-readiness.

12   Social Security Administration, Fact Sheet on Disability Benefits, 2024, https://blog.ssa.gov/understanding-social-security-disability-benefits/.

13   American Psychological Association, Marriage and Divorce Statistics, https://www.apa.org/monitor/2013/04/marriage.

14   Noam Wasserman, *The Founder's Dilemmas* (Harvard Business Review Press, 2012).

15   Federal Emergency Management Agency, Disaster Recovery and Resilience Statistics, 2023, https://emilms.fema.gov/is_0111a/groups/23.html.

16   Bill Perkins, *Die with Zero: Getting All You Can from Your Money and Your Life* (HarperBusiness, 2020).

17   Moshe A. Milevsky, *The 7 Most Important Equations for Your Retirement: The Fascinating People and Ideas Behind Planning Your Retirement Income* (Wiley, 2012).

18   Forbes Top Next-Gen Wealth Advisors Best-in-State for Florida in 2023 and 2024, published in August each year, research by SHOOK Research LLC, data as of March of the same year. Compensation provided for using, not obtaining, the rating. The rating is not based on quality of investment advice, investment performance, or client feedback.

ACKNOWLEDGMENTS

First and foremost, I want to express my sincere gratitude to my parents, Stylianos "Steve" and Cheri. Growing up in a household where hard work was the norm and every lesson came with a story or a moment of laughter shaped the way I see the world. With her meticulous coupon clipping and commitment to making the most of every resource, my mom showed me that careful planning and discipline can make a profound difference. My dad's encouragement to save part of every dollar earned, whether it was mowing lawns or bussing tables, taught me that small, consistent efforts lay the groundwork for bigger successes. His humor and endless tales could fill a book of their own, and I hope a touch of that spirit finds its way into these pages.

To my wife, Kristin: Your support and love are my greatest source of strength. With you by my side, I feel empowered to take on any challenge, big or small. Your belief in me fuels my passion and determination every single day.

I am also thankful for Judy Hall, a high school friend's mother who first opened my eyes to the world of financial advising. Her influence ignited a spark of curiosity about the financial world, one that grew into a passion for helping others achieve their dreams—a career that allows me to create a lasting impact by transforming lives and shaping family legacies for generations. To Joe Gitto, my fellow Exit Planning

Institute (EPI) chapter board member and friend—thank you for urging me to take the leap and write this book. Your encouragement kept me focused and motivated.

A big thank-you to the many friends, colleagues, and family members who took the time to review and proofread this book. Your feedback and honesty helped keep me grounded and ensured that my ideas stayed clear and relatable.

To my clients: Your trust is something I treasure. Working with you has been more than just a professional journey—it has been personal, filled with shared stories, challenges, and growth. Many of you feel like family to me, and it's been an honor to be part of your financial journey. This book is for you as much as anyone, and I hope it reflects the lessons and values we've discovered together.

And to you, the reader: My hope is that the insights in these pages help you make the most of your wealth, not just in numbers but in the experiences and impact it creates. Money is a tool, and when used thoughtfully, it can transform your journey into one of purpose, fulfillment, and lasting memories. I hope these insights empower you to share this same impact with your friends and family, fostering a ripple effect of positive change. Thank you all for being part of this journey—your support means everything.

ABOUT THE AUTHOR

George is a first-generation Greek American and a 2023 and 2024 Forbes Best-in-State Top Next-Gen Wealth Advisor.[18] As a University of Central Florida alumnus and avid football fan, George brings a unique perspective to the world of personal finance.

Alongside his roles as a devoted husband to Kristin and father to Ella and Aubrey, George is a CERTIFIED FINANCIAL PLANNER™ professional (CFP®) who also holds the following advanced credentials: Certified Exit Planning Advisor® (CEPA®), Certified Private Wealth Advisor® (CPWA®), Accredited Asset Management Specialist℠ (AAMS®), Chartered Retirement Plans Specialist℠ (CRPSS®), and Chartered Retirement Planning Counselor℠ (CRPC®). Drawing on over fifteen years of experience and thousands of diverse client interactions, George has developed a talent for humanizing finance, helping clients navigate the complexities of wealth management while empowering both investors and advisors.

In *Two-Comma Wealth*, George shares the lessons and wisdom he has accumulated throughout his career, aiming to guide readers toward building, distributing, and preserving substantial personal wealth. An open book by nature, George thrives on connecting with others and providing a personalized touch to the financial planning process. Learn more about George at twocommawealth.com.